Shakespeare
on Stage and Screen

Romeo and Juliet
in Excerpts

edited by

Rainer Gocke and Marlena Tronicke

Series Editors

Rainer Gocke and Franziska Quabeck

Schöningh
westermann

© 2016 Bildungshaus Schulbuchverlage
Westermann Schroedel Diesterweg Schöningh Winklers GmbH
Braunschweig, Paderborn, Darmstadt

www.verlage.westermanngruppe.de/schoeningh
Schöningh Verlag, Jühenplatz 1–3, 33098 Paderborn

Druck A 5 4 3 2 1 / Jahr 2020 19 18 17 16
Alle Drucke der Serie A sind im Unterricht parallel verwendbar.
Die letzte Zahl bezeichnet das Jahr dieses Druckes.

Umschlaggestaltung: Nora Krull, Bielefeld
Umschlagabbildung: © COLLECTION CHRISTOPHEL / action press
Druck und Bindung: westermann druck GmbH, Braunschweig

ISBN 978-3-14-040268-2

Contents

An asterisk* behind a word in the questions or the commentary means that it is explained in the Glossary at the end of the book.

And ... Action!

Although not part of the so-called 'great tragedies' (*Hamlet, Othello, King Lear,* and *Macbeth*), *Romeo and Juliet* is one of Shakespeare's most popular plays. The central couple are the most famous lovers in literature, and even without having read the play, almost every schoolchild knows the plot and its tragic ending. Although set in late medieval Italy, Shakespeare's portrayal of young love has proven a timeless tale. In this context, it is often overlooked just how young the lovers are: Juliet has not yet celebrated her fourteenth birthday, and Romeo is believed to be only slightly older.

Of course the play investigates other themes such as the double-sidedness of love more generally as well as hatred, fate, and the role of time. Because of such universal topics, *Romeo and Juliet* is still one of the most frequently performed plays. Both stage and screen productions have reimagined and updated it countless times, and it has been relocated to various historical and cultural backgrounds. Famously, Leonard Bernstein's musical *West Side Story* sets the story in late 1950s Manhattan. The feud between the houses of Montague and Capulet here becomes a street war between the American gang the 'Jets' and their Puerto Rican rival, the 'Sharks'.

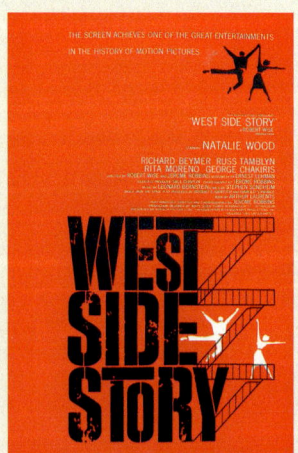

Dir. Robert Wise and Jerome Robbins, music by Leonard Bernstein, Natalie Wood and Richard Beymer (1961)

Dir. Franco Zeffirelli, starring Olivia Hussey and Leonard Whiting (1968)

Dir. Kelly Asbury, voices by Emily Blunt and James McAvoy (2011)

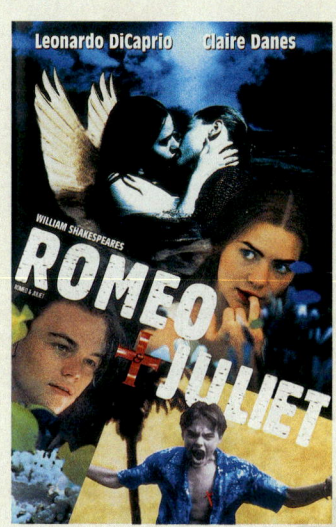

Dir. Baz Luhrmann, starring Claire Danes
and Leonardo DiCaprio (1996)

Any form of production, either on stage or screen, is always an act of interpretation. With film this is especially important since this medium has much more and rather different visual, audiovisual and sound techniques to portray the characters, introduce motifs* or symbols, and create settings*. Baz Luhrmann's blockbuster film *William Shakespeare's Romeo + Juliet*, starring Claire Danes and Leonardo DiCaprio, is one of the most successful screen adaptations of Shakespeare's plays. Luhrmann transports the play to the fictional 'Verona Beach', home to a war between two mafia gangs. In contrast to this modern interpretation of the setting, he keeps the original text and merely shortens it. Luhrmann is generally known for a very innovative use of music. When watching extracts from the film, pay special attention to what role music plays here, too.

Activities

1. Watch the first chapter of Baz Luhrmann's *Romeo + Juliet* and pay attention to the following details: What does this exposition* tell us about the setting?

2. What, according to this opening sequence, is the film's central conflict? What information do we get concerning the central character constellations?

Central Character Constellations

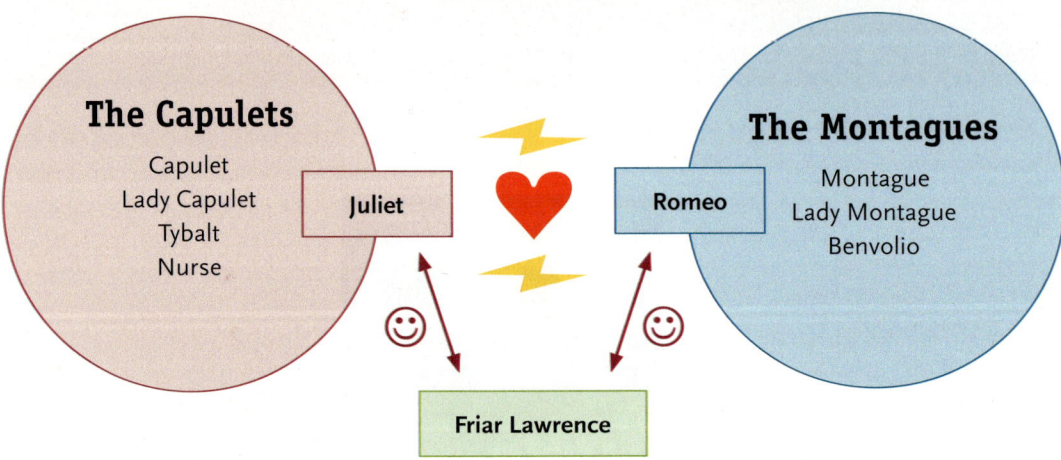

The Capulets

Capulet
Lady Capulet
Tybalt
Nurse

Juliet

Romeo

The Montagues

Montague
Lady Montague
Benvolio

Friar Lawrence

The Court

The Prince of Verona
Mercutio, the Prince's cousin and Romeo's friend
Paris, the Prince's cousin and Juliet's suitor

Leonardo DiCaprio and Claire Danes in Baz Luhrmann's film adaption (1996)

Romeo and Juliet

The Prologue

1

Enter CHORUS.

CHORUS Two households, both alike in dignity,
   In fair Verona (where we lay our scene),
   From ancient grudge break to new mutiny,
   Where civil blood makes civil hands unclean.
5 From forth the fatal loins of these two foes
   A pair of star-crossed lovers take their life;
   Whose misadventured piteous overthrows
   Doth with their death bury their parents' strife.
   The fearful passage of their death-marked love,
10 And the continuance of their parents' rage,
   Which but their children's end nought could remove,
   Is now the two hours' traffic of our stage;
   The which if you with patient ears attend,
   What here shall miss, our toil shall strive to mend.

Exit

both ... dignity the one as noble as the other
grudge long-term hatred
mutiny disorder, violence
civil blood the blood of other citizens of Verona
from ... loins as offsprings
star-crossed ill-fated, unlucky
take their life are born
misadventured unfortunate
overthrows tragic accidents
strife conflict
fearful passage terrible course
death-marked doomed to death
but apart from
nought nothing
remove bring to an end
traffic activity, performance
attend listen to
what ... miss that which I have left out in this prologue
toil acting

Activities

1. Check the following terms in various sources and apply your findings to Text 1: prologue*, chorus*, sonnet*.

2. Outline the structure of the present sonnet and describe the contents of its different parts.

3. Quote and explain all terms referring to a theatre performance.

4. Re-watch the first chapter of the movie. What effect is created by having the Prologue spoken by a news anchor on TV? Why do you think are the words repeated by the voiceover* in the following sequence?

5. What function does the flashforward* at the end of the sequence have?

Act 1

Act 1 – Scene 1

2

LADY MONTAGUE O where is Romeo? saw you him today?
   Right glad I am he was not at this fray.

BENVOLIO Madam, an hour before the worshipped sun
   Peered forth the golden window of the east,
   A troubled mind drive me to walk abroad,   5
   Where underneath the grove of sycamore,
   That westward rooteth from this city side,
   So early walking did I see your son;
   Towards him I made, but he was ware of me,
   And stole into the covert of the wood;   10
   I, measuring his affections by my own,
   Which then most sought where most might not be found,
   Being one too many by my weary self,
   Pursued my humour, not pursuing his,
   And gladly shunned who gladly fled from me.   15

MONTAGUE Many a morning hath he there been seen,
   With tears augmenting the fresh morning's dew,
   Adding to clouds more clouds with his deep sighs,
   But all so soon as the all-cheering sun
   Should in the farthest east begin to draw   20
   The shady curtains from Aurora's bed,
   Away from light steals home my heavy son,
   And private in his chamber pens himself,
   Shuts up his windows, locks fair daylight out,
   And makes himself an artificial night: 25
   Black and portentous must this humour prove,
   Unless good counsel may the cause remove.

BENVOLIO My noble uncle, do you know the cause?

MONTAGUE I neither know it, nor can learn of him.

BENVOLIO Have you importuned him by any means?   30

MONTAGUE Both by myself and many other friends,
   But he, his own affections' counsellor,
   Is to himself (I will not say how true)
   But to himself so secret and so close,
   So far from sounding and discovery,   35
   As is the bud bit with an envious worm
   Ere he can spread his sweet leaves to the air,
   Or dedicate his beauty to the sun.
   Could we but learn from whence his sorrows grow,
   We would as willingly give cure as know.   40

---

drive drove
to walk abroad to leave the house
sycamore a tree; maybe a play on words 'sick amour'
was ware became aware of me
stole ... wood hid in the wood
affections feelings
Which ... found which desired a place, now and then, where I could be alone
Being one ... self having enough of myself
Pursued ... from me I did what he wanted me to do, i.e. left him to himself and did not intrude on him
augmenting doubling

Aurora goddess of the dawn in ancient mythology
heavy very sad
pens himself shuts himself away from the sunny morning

portentous ill-omened

importuned asked

close quiet

he it
his its

as willingly ... know help him forget his sadness and find the cause for it

Enter ROMEO.

BENVOLIO See where he comes. So please you step aside,
I'll know his grievance or be much denied.

I'll know ... denied I'll find out
what he grieves about if he is
willing to tell me

MONTAGUE I would thou wert so happy by thy stay
To hear true shrift. Come, madam, let's away.

I would ... true shrift I hope you
succeed in his telling you the
truth about it

Exeunt MONTAGUE *and* LADY MONTAGUE

45 BENVOLIO Good morrow, cousin.

ROMEO   Is the day so young?

BENVOLIO But new struck nine.

ROMEO   Ay me, sad hours seem long.
Was that my father that went hence so fast?

BENVOLIO It was. What sadness lengthens Romeo's hours?

ROMEO Not having that, which, having, makes them short.

50 BENVOLIO In love?

ROMEO Out –

BENVOLIO Of love?

ROMEO Out of her favour where I am in love.

BENVOLIO Alas that Love, so gentle in his view,
55   Should be so tyrannous and rough in proof!

'Here's much to do with hate,
but more with love'
(dir. Baz Luhrmann, 1996)

ROMEO Alas that Love, whose view is muffled still,
Should, without eyes, see pathways to his will!
Where shall we dine? O me! what fray was here?
Yet tell me not, for I have heard it all:
60   Here's much to do with hate, but more with love:
Why then, O brawling love, O loving hate,
O any thing of nothing first create!
O heavy lightness, serious vanity,
Misshapen chaos of well-seeming forms,

rough in proof harsh in
experience
whose view ... still, which is
blind
should ... will should never-
theless get its own way

Here's much ... love the people
fighting each other seem to have
enjoyed the fight even more
than I am unhappy in my love
create created

Feather of lead, bright smoke, cold fire, sick health,
Still-waking sleep, that is not what it is!
This love feel I, that feel no love in this.   65

This love … in this I feel
completely unhappy (concerning my love to Rosaline)

Activities

1.   Before an important character appears for the first time, Shakespeare often makes others talk about the new figure. Give reasons as to why this might be so.

2.   How do we know who is on stage when we watch or listen to the play without reading the stage-directions*?

3.   What are your first impressions of Romeo? How is he seen by his parents and by Benvolio, his cousin? What impression do you get from his own speeches?

4.   Comment on aspects of the characters' language which you find remarkable.

5.   Watch chapter 02 until 0:13:03 of the running time. How is Romeo introduced? How does this compare to Romeo's introduction in the play?

6.   This is the first passage of proper dialogue. What effect is created by the contrast between the modern images and Shakespeare's original lines?

Act 1 – Scene 2

Paris asks Capulet for the hand of his daughter. Capulet hesitates but still invites Paris to the annual ball. As a Montague, Romeo is not allowed to attend but still wants to go in the hope of meeting a lot of pretty women.

Act 1 – Scene 3

3

Nurse   Thou wast the prettiest babe that e'er I nursed.
And I might live to see thee married once,
I have my wish.

once one day

LADY CAPULET Marry, that 'marry' is the very theme
5   I came to talk of. Tell me, daughter Juliet,
     How stands your dispositions to be married?

JULIET It is an honour that I dream not of.

NURSE An honour! were not I thine only nurse,
     I would say thou hadst sucked wisdom from thy teat.

10 LADY CAPULET Well, think of marriage now; younger than you,
     Here in Verona, ladies of esteem,
     Are made already mothers. By my count,
     I was your mother much upon these years
     That you are now a maid. Thus then in brief:
15   The valiant Paris seeks you for his love.

NURSE A man, young lady! lady, such a man
     As all the world – Why, he's a man of wax.

LADY CAPULET Verona's summer hath not such a flower.

NURSE Nay, he's a flower, in faith, a very flower.

20 LADY CAPULET What say you, can you love the gentleman?
     This night you shall behold him at our feast;
     Read o'er the volume of young Paris' face,
     And find delight writ there with beauty's pen;
     Examine every married lineament,
25   And see how one another lends content;
     And what obscured in this fair volume lies
     Find written in the margent of his eyes.
     This precious book of love, this unbound lover,
     To beautify him, only lacks a cover.
30   The fish lives in the sea, and 'tis much pride
     For fair without the fair within to hide;
     That book in many's eyes doth share the glory
     That in gold clasps locks in the golden story:
     So shall you share all that he doth possess,
35   By having him, making yourself no less.

How ... married what do you think of getting married?

from thy teat from the teat that sucked you

by my count as far as I am concerned

'Well, think of marriage now' (dir. Franco Zeffirelli, 1968)

man of wax rather ideal, good-looking man

Read o'er ... face look carefully in his face
find delight ... pen find in his looks a promise of happiness to come
every married lineament all his harmonious features
one ... content they complement each other
margent margin
This precious ... cover Paris is compared by Lady Capulet to a book which only needs a cover, i.e. a wife to love him
and 'tis ... hide and it is a wife's pride to be the centre of her lover's admiration
That book ... story so Juliet will be like the binding of a book that will share the value of its contents, i.e. her husband's honour
no less his equal

women ... men women are made pregnant by men
like of be pleased with
I'll ... move I will find out if looking leads to liking
But no more ... fly But I won't do more than you expect me to do

NURSE No less! nay, bigger women grow by men.

LADY CAPULET Speak briefly, can you like of Paris' love?

JULIET I'll look to like, if looking liking move;
But no more deep will I endart mine eye
Than your consent gives strength to make it fly.   40

Activities

1. Describe your first impression of the three characters* on stage.

2. If you were to perform the play or parts of it, which of the three ladies would you like to play?

3. Which of the images and word-plays do you find noteworthy and why?

4. Watch chapter 05 of the DVD. How is Juliet introduced? What kind of relationship does she have with her mother?

Act 1 – Scene 4

Before attending the ball, Romeo and his friends meet in front of the Capulets' house. Everyone is excited, but Romeo feels depressed. Mercutio tries to cheer him up with the story of Queen Mab, a fairy who brings dreams. Romeo says that he feels something awful will happen that night.

Act 1 – Scene 5

4

ROMEO [*To a Servingman*] What lady's that which doth enrich the hand
Of yonder knight?

SERVINGMAN I know not, sir.

Ethiop's ear African's ear
Beauty ... dear her beauty is too valuable for this earth
So shows ... crows she is a white dove among crows
fellows friends

ROMEO O she doth teach the torches to burn bright!
It seems she hangs upon the cheek of night   5
As a rich jewel in an Ethiop's ear –
Beauty too rich for use, for earth too dear:
So shows a snowy dove trooping with crows,
As yonder lady o'er her fellows shows.

10 The measure done, I'll watch her place of stand,
And touching hers, make blessèd my rude hand.
Did my heart love till now? forswear it, sight!
For I ne'er saw true beauty till this night.

TYBALT This, by his voice, should be a Montague.
15 Fetch me my rapier, boy.

Exit PAGE

What dares the slave
Come hither, covered with an antic face,
To fleer and scorn at our solemnity?
Now by the stock and honour of my kin,
To strike him dead I hold it not a sin.

20 CAPULET Why, how now, kinsman, wherefore storm you so?

TYBALT Uncle, this is a Montague, our foe:
A villain that is hither come in spite,
To scorn at our solemnity this night.

CAPULET Young Romeo is it?

TYBALT 'Tis he, that villain Romeo.

25 CAPULET Content thee, gentle coz, let him alone,
'A bears him like a portly gentleman;
And to say truth, Verona brags of him
To be a virtuous and well-governed youth.
I would not for the wealth of all this town
30 Here in my house do him disparagement;
Therefore be patient, take no note of him;
It is my will, the which if thou respect,
Show a fair presence, and put off these frowns,
An ill-beseeming semblance for a feast.

35 TYBALT It fits when such a villain is a guest:
I'll not endure him.

The measure ... stand I'll watch carefully where she stands as soon as the dance is over
forswear deny

antic face grotesque mask
fleer mock
solemnity feast, celebration
Now ... kin by the honour of my family and my ancestors

wherefore ... so why are you so enraged?

content thee calm down
'A bears ... gentleman he behaves like a well-educated gentleman
well-governed sensible
do him disparagement I will not speak ill of him
note notice
the which ... respect which I order you to respect
Show ... presence behave cheerfully
ill-beseeming ... feast as it is inappropriate for our feast

'This, by his voice, should be a Montague' (dir. Baz Luhrmann, 1996)

CAPULET He shall be endured.
What, goodman boy, I say he shall, go to!
Am I the master here, or you? go to!
You'll not endure him? God shall mend my soul,
You'll make a mutiny among my guests!   40
You will set cock-a-hoop! you'll be the man!

TYBALT Why, uncle, 'tis a shame.

CAPULET Go to, go to,
You are a saucy boy. Is't so indeed?
This trick may chance to scathe you, I know what.
You must contrary me! Marry, 'tis time. –   45
Well said, my hearts! – You are a princox, go,
Be quiet, or – More light, more light! – For shame,
I'll make you quiet, what! – Cheerly, my hearts!

TYBALT Patience perforce with wilful choler meeting
Makes my flesh tremble in their different greeting: 50
I will withdraw, but this intrusion shall,
Now seeming sweet, convert to bitt'rest gall.   *Exit*

ROMEO [*To* JULIET] If I profane with my unworthiest hand
This holy shrine, the gentle sin is this,
My lips, two blushing pilgrims, ready stand   55
To smooth that rough touch with a tender kiss.

JULIET Good pilgrim, you do wrong your hand too much,
Which mannerly devotion shows in this,
For saints have hands that pilgrims' hands do touch,
And palm to palm is holy palmers' kiss.   60

ROMEO Have not saints lips, and holy palmers too?

JULIET Ay, pilgrim, lips that they must use in prayer.

ROMEO O then, dear saint, let lips do what hands do:
They pray, grant thou, lest faith turn to despair.

JULIET Saints do not move, though grant for prayers' sake.   65

---

goodman boy do as I tell you, you insolent boy (Capulet reacts angrily as Tybalt is unwilling to obey him)

You … man You will run riot! You will show you are the boss, ha!

saucy impertinent
This trick … you your behaviour may get you into trouble
You … time You want to defy me? I think it's time …
princox insolent young man
cheerly, my hearts well-done, dear friends

Patience … meeting patience overruling my overwhelming anger
in … greeting because of my opposing feelings
gall poison
profane abuse
This holy shrine your maiden hand
My lips … pilgrims my lips like pilgrims on their way to Jerusalem
Which … this It only shows true devotion
And palm … kiss so putting (our) hands together resembles a kiss proper to pilgrims

dear saint dear Juliet
They pray … despair my lips pray, "give me a kiss; if not – my faith in you may turn into despair"
Saints … sake a saint's statue does not move but may grant prayers

'Have not saints lips …?' (dir. Baz Luhrmann, 1996)

ROMEO Then move not while my prayer's effect I take.
Thus from my lips, by thine, my sin is purged.
Kissing her.

JULIET Then have my lips the sin that they have took.

ROMEO Sin from my lips? O trespass sweetly urged!
70   Give me my sin again.
Kissing her again.

JULIET   You kiss by th'book.

NURSE Madam, your mother craves a word with you.

ROMEO What is her mother?

NURSE   Marry, bachelor,
Her mother is the lady of the house,
And a good lady, and a wise and virtuous.
75   I nursed her daughter that you talked withal;
I tell you, he that can lay hold of her
Shall have the chinks.

ROMEO   Is she a Capulet?
O dear account! my life is my foe's debt.

BENVOLIO Away, be gone, the sport is at the best.

80 **ROMEO** Ay, so I fear, the more is my unrest.

CAPULET Nay, gentlemen, prepare not to be gone,
We have a trifling foolish banquet towards.
They whisper in his ear.
Is it e'en so? Why then I thank you all.
I thank you, honest gentlemen, good night.
85   More torches here, come on! then let's to bed.
Ah, sirrah, by my fay, it waxes late,
I'll to my rest.
Exeunt all but JULIET *and* NURSE

JULIET Come hither, Nurse. What is yond gentleman?

NURSE The son and heir of old Tiberio.

90 **JULIET** What's he that now is going out of door?

NURSE Marry, that I think be young Petruchio.

JULIET What's he that follows here, that would not dance?

NURSE I know not.

JULIET Go ask his name. – If he be marrièd,
95   My grave is like to be my wedding bed.

NURSE His name is Romeo, and a Montague,
The only son of your great enemy.

---

while ... take while I try to get a kiss
purged washed away

O trespass ... urged You sweetly urged me to commit this sin

You ... book you seem to know a lot about this subject
craves ... you would like to talk to you

withal with

he that ... chinks he that marries her will get a lot of money

O dear ... debt what a dire story, I'm at my enemy's mercy
the sport ... best it's high time to leave

We have ... towards there are light refreshments left for you – just arrived

honest honourable

fay faith
waxes grows

What ... gentleman who is this gentleman over there

My grave ... bed I will die a virgin

My only ... hate he whom I love comes from the family I hate
Too early ... late I regret having fallen in love with him before I knew him
Prodigious ill-omened

JULIET My only love sprung from my only hate!
　　Too early seen unknown, and known too late!
　　Prodigious birth of love it is to me,　　　　　100
　　That I must love a loathèd enemy.

Activities

1. Subdivide the text into four sections and give a headline to each of them.

2. Compare Romeo's enthusiastic description of Juliet with Lady Capulet's praise of Count Paris (Text 3).

3. Explain the dramatic functions of the dialogue between Capulet and Tybalt.

4. Describe the artificial first dialogue of the two lovers.

5. What are the consequences of the revealed family ties?

6. Watch chapters 08 and 09 of the DVD. Romeo and Juliet's first meeting involves a rather interesting prop*. Think about the possible symbolism of the aquarium in this scene.

7. Like in the play, the first meeting takes place at a costume ball. Why do you think the director has chosen these particular costumes for Romeo, Juliet, and Tybalt?

8. Watch chapter 12. How do the mise-en-scène* and camera movement* capture the couple's shock when they notice that the other is a member of the rival family?

Act 2

Act 2 – Scene 1

In this scene, Benvolio and Mercutio are looking for Romeo, who seems to have disappeared. They make fun of Romeo's love-sickness because they think that being in love is rather old-fashioned.

Act 2 – Scene 2

5

In the meantime, Romeo has arrived at the Capulets' garden. He secretly watches Juliet standing on the balcony, and when he hears her confessing her love for him he makes his presence known.

ROMEO O wilt thou leave me so unsatisfied?

JULIET What satisfaction canst thou have tonight?

ROMEO Th'exchange of thy love's faithful vow for mine.

JULIET I gave thee mine before thou didst request it;
5   And yet I would it were to give again.

> **And yet … again** nevertheless I wish I had it back to give it then again

ROMEO Wouldst thou withdraw it? for what purpose, love?

JULIET But to be frank and give it thee again,
And yet I wish but for the thing I have:
My bounty is as boundless as the sea,
10   My love as deep; the more I give to thee
The more I have, for both are infinite.

> **But … frank** only to be generous
> **And yet … I have** I am begging for what I already have
> **bounty** generosity

Nurse calls within.

I hear some noise within; dear love, adieu! –
Anon, good Nurse! – Sweet Montague, be true.
Stay but a little, I will come again.   *Exit above*

> **Anon** I'm coming; at once
> **Stay … little** just a minute, please
> **I am afeard** I fear

15 ROMEO O blessèd, blessèd night! I am afeard,
Being in night, all this is but a dream,
Too flattering-sweet to be substantial.

Enter JULIET above.

JULIET Three words, dear Romeo, and good night indeed.
If that thy bent of love be honourable,
20   Thy purpose marriage, send me word tomorrow,

> **If that … honourable** if your intention of wooing me is honourable

procure authorise
rite ceremony of marriage

By one that I'll procure to come to thee,
Where and what time thou wilt perform the rite,
And all my fortunes at thy foot I'll lay,
And follow thee my lord throughout the world.

NURSE [*Within*] Madam! 25

But if ... well but if your
intentions are not honourable
I do beseech thee I beg you

JULIET I come, anon. – But if thou meanest not well,
I do beseech thee –

NURSE [*Within*]   Madam!

To cease thy strife to stop this
courtship

JULIET   By and by I come –
To cease thy strife, and leave me to my grief.
Tomorrow will I send.

ROMEO So thrive my soul – 30

JULIET   A thousand times good night!

Exit above

to want to miss; to be without

ROMEO A thousand times the worse, to want thy light.
Love goes toward love as schoolboys from their books,
But love from love, toward school with heavy looks.
Retiring slowly.

Enter JULIET *again above.*

Love goes ... heavy looks a lover
is as much attracted by his
beloved person as schoolboys
detest their schoolbooks; love
abstains from love as much as
schoolboys go to school
unwillingly
Hist! Psst
for a falconer's voice I wish I
could get him back using a
falconer's voice (falconer lured
the bird with his sweet tone of
voice)
tassel-gentle a highly prized
male falcon
Bondage is hoarse I am under
control in this house so I can
only whisper
Else would ... Echo lies
otherwise I would tear open the
cave where the Goddess Echo
lies
tongue voice
soul love
attending listening

JULIET Hist, Romeo, hist! O for a falc'ner's voice,
To lure this tassel-gentle back again: 35
Bondage is hoarse, and may not speak aloud,
Else would I tear the cave where Echo lies,
And make her airy tongue more hoarse than mine
With repetition of my Romeo's name.

ROMEO It is my soul that calls upon my name. 40
How silver-sweet sound lovers' tongues by night,
Like softest music to attending ears!

'How silver-sweet sound
lovers' tongues by night'
(dir. Robert Wise, 1961)

JULIET Romeo!

ROMEO   My niësse?

niësse my sweet hawk

JULIET   What a'clock tomorrow
    Shall I send to thee?

ROMEO   By the hour of nine.

45 JULIET I will not fail, 'tis twenty year till then.
    I have forgot why I did call thee back.

ROMEO Let me stand here till thou remember it.

JULIET I shall forget, to have thee still stand there,
    Rememb'ring how I love thy company.

I shall forget I will deliberately
forget
Remembering reminding
myself of

50 ROMEO And I'll still stay, to have thee still forget,
    Forgetting any other home but this.

JULIET 'Tis almost morning, I would have thee gone:
    And yet no farther than a wanton's bird,
    That lets it hop a little from his hand,

a wanton's bird the bird a spoilt
child can play with

55 Like a poor prisoner in his twisted gyves,
    And with a silken thread plucks it back again,
    So loving-jealous of his liberty.

gyves ropes

ROMEO I would I were thy bird.

I would I wish

JULIET   Sweet, so would I,
    Yet I should kill thee with much cherishing.
60 Good night, good night! Parting is such sweet sorrow,
    That I shall say good night till it be morrow.   *Exit above*

ROMEO Sleep dwell upon thine eyes, peace in thy breast!
    Would I were sleep and peace, so sweet to rest!

Activities

1. The final phase of the famous balcony scene abounds in
        mutual declarations of love. Choose some of them which you
        find most impressive and justify your choice.

2. Some readers or spectators might find the abundance of
        such declarations too sentimental. By what means does
        Shakespeare try to avoid this impression?

3. Watch chapter 14 from 0:35:00 — end. Compare the famous
        balcony scene in the play to that in the film. Are there any
        differences in tone?

4. What could be possible reasons for making most of the scene
        take place in a pool? How does water relate to Romeo and
        Juliet's relationship?

Act 2 – Scene 3

6

ROMEO Good morrow, father.

FRIAR LAWRENCE   Benedicite!
  What early tongue so sweet saluteth me?
  Young son, it argues a distempered head
  So soon to bid good morrow to thy bed:
  Care keeps his watch in every old man's eye,   5
  And where care lodges, sleep will never lie;
  But where unbruisèd youth with unstuffed brain
  Doth couch his limbs, there golden sleep doth reign.
  Therefore thy earliness doth me assure
  Thou art uprousèd with some distemp'rature;   10
  Or if not so, then here I hit it right,
  Our Romeo hath not been in bed tonight.

ROMEO That last is true, the sweeter rest was mine.

FRIAR LAWRENCE God pardon sin! wast thou with Rosaline?

ROMEO With Rosaline, my ghostly father? no;   15
  I have forgot that name, and that name's woe.

FRIAR LAWRENCE That's my good son, but where hast thou been
  then?

ROMEO I'll tell thee ere thou ask it me again:
  I have been feasting with mine enemy,
  Where on a sudden one hath wounded me   20
  That's by me wounded; both our remedies
  Within thy help and holy physic lies.
  I bear no hatred, blessèd man; for lo,
  My intercession likewise steads my foe.

FRIAR LAWRENCE Be plain, good son, and homely in thy drift,   25
  Riddling confession finds but riddling shrift.

ROMEO Then plainly know, my heart's dear love is set
  On the fair daughter of rich Capulet;
  As mine on hers, so hers is set on mine,
  And all combined, save what thou must combine   30
  By holy marriage. When and where and how
  We met, we wooed, and made exchange of vow,
  I'll tell thee as we pass, but this I pray,
  That thou consent to marry us today.

FRIAR LAWRENCE Holy Saint Francis, what a change is here!   35
  Is Rosaline, that thou didst love so dear,
  So soon forsaken? Young men's love then lies
  Not truly in their hearts, but in their eyes.

Benedicite God be with you
early tongue early riser
argues ... head shows a disturbed state of mind

unbruised inexperienced
unstuffed not troubled

uproused ... distemperature woken up by bad dreams
hit it right suggest correctly

one someone
both our remedies the cure for both of us
holy physic religious remedy (i.e. marriage)
intercession request
steads helps
homely ... drift clear in what you say
Riddling ... shrift if your confession is a riddle you will get an unsatisfactory absolution

And all ... combine and as we both have agreed (to get married) help us in our plan
pass walk along
pray beg of you

but in their eyes in their outward appearance

Jesu Maria, what a deal of brine
40   Hath washed thy sallow cheeks for Rosaline!
How much salt water thrown away in waste,
To season love, that of it doth not taste!
The sun not yet thy sighs from heaven clears,
Thy old groans yet ringing in mine ancient ears;
45   Lo here upon thy cheek the stain doth sit
Of an old tear that is not washed off yet.
If e'er thou wast thyself, and these woes thine,
Thou and these woes were all for Rosaline.

And art thou changed? Pronounce this sentence then:
50   Women may fall, when there's no strength in men.

ROMEO Thou chid'st me oft for loving Rosaline.

FRIAR LAWRENCE For doting, not for loving, pupil mine.

ROMEO And bad'st me bury love.

FRIAR LAWRENCE   Not in a grave,
To lay one in, another out to have.

55 ROMEO I pray thee chide me not. Her I love now
Doth grace for grace and love for love allow;
The other did not so.

FRIAR LAWRENCE   O she knew well
Thy love did read by rote, that could not spell.
But come, young waverer, come go with me,
60   In one respect I'll thy assistant be:
For this alliance may so happy prove
To turn your households' rancour to pure love.

ROMEO O let us hence, I stand on sudden haste.

FRIAR LAWRENCE Wisely and slow, they stumble that run fast.

Exeunt

what … brine how many tears

To season … not taste to preserve love that does not taste of love
The sun … clears we still hear your sighs
Lo … sit Look there's still a tear drop on your cheek

And … changed and have you really changed?
Women … men women may be excused for committing a sin when men are weak

To lay … to have to bury one lover in order to start a new love affair
Her I … allow she I love now loves me as well

Thy love … spell that you quoted words of love from books without understanding what you said
In one respect for one reason
rancour hatred

stand … haste must act quickly now

'For this alliance may
so happy prove'
(dir. Franco Zeffirelli, 1968)

Activities

1. Give possible reasons as to why Shakespeare wrote the whole of the present dialogue in rhymes.

2. There are quite a few examples of proverbial wisdom in this passage. Find and explain them.

3. To a certain extent this passage presents a comic clash between contrasting characters. Elaborate on this.

4. In how far is the plot of the play developed in this text?

5. Watch chapter 15 of the DVD. Friar Lawrence represents the institution of the Church. What image of him is conveyed in this scene?

6. What, according to this scene, is the friar's motivation for helping Romeo?

Act 2 – Scene 4

This scene informs us about the rivalry between Mercutio and Tybalt. Tybalt, we learn, is very keen on weapons, especially rapiers. This is a very bawdy scene, full of sexual undertones. Also, Romeo gives the nurse details about their wedding preparations.

Act 2 – Scene 5
Capulet's mansion

7

Enter JULIET.

JULIET The clock struck nine when I did send the Nurse;
In half an hour she promised to return.
Perchance she cannot meet him: that's not so.
O, she is lame! Love's heralds should be thoughts,
Which ten times faster glides than the sun's beams,   5
Driving back shadows over low'ring hills;
Therefore do nimble-pinioned doves draw Love,
And therefore hath the wind-swift Cupid wings.
Now is the sun upon the highmost hill
Of this day's journey, and from nine till twelve   10
Is three long hours, yet she is not come.

lame slow

low'ring dark, gloomy
nimble-pinion'd doves
swift-winged doves (sacred to Venus)
highmost hill meridian

Had she affections and warm youthful blood,
She would be as swift in motion as a ball;
My words would bandy her to my sweet love,
15   And his to me.
But old folks, many feign as they were dead,
Unwieldy, slow, heavy, and pale as lead.

Enter NURSE *with* PETER.

O God, she comes! O honey Nurse, what news?
Hast thou met with him? Send thy man away.

20 NURSE Peter, stay at the gate.

Exit PETER

JULIET Now, good sweet Nurse – O Lord, why look'st thou sad?
Though news be sad, yet tell them merrily;
If good, thou shamest the music of sweet news
By playing it to me with so sour a face.

25 NURSE I am a-weary, give me leave a while.
Fie, how my bones ache! What a jaunce have I!

JULIET I would thou hadst my bones, and I thy news.
Nay, come, I pray thee speak, good, good Nurse, speak.

NURSE Jesu, what haste! can you not stay a while?
30   Do you not see that I am out of breath?

JULIET How art thou out of breath, when thou hast breath
To say to me that thou art out of breath?
The excuse that thou dost make in this delay
Is longer than the tale thou dost excuse.
35   Is thy news good or bad? Answer to that.
Say either, and I'll stay the circumstance:
Let me be satisfied, is't good or bad?

NURSE Well, you have made a simple choice, you know not how to
choose a man: Romeo? no, not he; though his face be better
40   than any man's, yet his leg excels all men's, and for a hand and a
foot and a body, though they be not to be talked on, yet they are
past compare. He is not the flower of courtesy, but I'll warrant
him, as gentle as a lamb. Go thy ways, wench, serve God. What,
have you dined at home?

45 JULIET No, no! But all this did I know before.
What says he of our marriage, what of that?

NURSE Lord, how my head aches! what a head have I!
It beats as it would fall in twenty pieces.
My back a't'other side – ah, my back, my back!
50   Beshrew your heart for sending me about
To catch my death with jauncing up and down!

---

bandy send her to and fro (like a ping-pong ball)

But old ... dead some old people pretend that they were not able to move

sad miserable
them the news
If good ... news if the news is good you deliver it with a very sour face
give ... awhile leave me alone for a moment
what a ... have I how tiring my journey was

stay awhile wait a moment

stay the circumstance wait for the details

simple foolish, silly

though they ... talked on although they are not worth mentioning
flower of courtesy behaving like a gentleman
I'll warrant ... lamb I tell you he is as gentle as a lamb

My back ... side my back is on the other side
Beshrew ... heart a curse on you!
with ... down by trudging back and forth

JULIET I'faith, I am sorry that thou art not well.
Sweet, sweet, sweet Nurse, tell me, what says my love?

NURSE Your love says, like an honest gentleman,
And a courteous, and a kind, and a handsome, 55
And I warrant a virtuous – Where is your mother?

JULIET Where is my mother? why, she is within,
Where should she be? How oddly thou repliest:
'Your love says, like an honest gentleman,
"Where is your mother?"' 60

O God's lady dear by the virgin Mary
hot keen, eager
poultice remedy

NURSE O God's lady dear,
Are you so hot? Marry come up, I trow;
Is this the poultice for my aching bones?
Henceforward do your messages yourself.

Here's ... coil What a fuss is this!

JULIET Here's such a coil! Come, what says Romeo?

NURSE Have you got leave to go to shrift today? 65

JULIET I have.

hie you hence off you go

NURSE Then hie you hence to Friar Lawrence' cell,
There stays a husband to make you a wife.

wanton rebellious

Now comes the wanton blood up in your cheeks,
They'll be in scarlet straight at any news. 70
Hie you to church, I must another way,
To fetch a ladder, by the which your love

a bird's nest into your room
I am ... delight now I am doing a job for you to make you happy

Must climb a bird's nest soon when it is dark.
I am the drudge, and toil in your delight;
But you shall bear the burden soon at night. 75
Go, I'll to dinner, hie you to the cell.

Hie to ... fortune now the wheel of fortune has brought me to its highest point

JULIET Hie to high fortune! Honest Nurse, farewell.

Exeunt

'But you shall bear the burden soon at night'
(dir. Franco Zeffirelli, 1968)

Activities

1. What is Juliet's dominating mood in this scene? How does she express it?

2. Have a closer look at the opening soliloquy*, her central ideas and the images expressing them.

3. How does the nurse behave? What are her intentions? What effects does she produce in Juliet and in the audience?

4. Watch chapter 18 of the DVD. How does this scene characterize the relationship between Juliet and the nurse?

Act 2 – Scene 6
Friar Lawrence's cell

Enter FRIAR LAWRENCE *and* ROMEO.

FRIAR LAWRENCE So smile the heavens upon this holy act,
    That after-hours with sorrow chide us not.

ROMEO Amen, amen! but come what sorrow can,
    It cannot countervail the exchange of joy
5   That one short minute gives me in her sight.
    Do thou but close our hands with holy words,
    Then love-devouring Death do what he dare,
    It is enough I may but call her mine.

FRIAR LAWRENCE These violent delights have violent ends,
10   And in their triumph die like fire and powder,
    Which as they kiss consume. The sweetest honey
    Is loathsome in his own deliciousness,
    And in the taste confounds the appetite.
    Therefore love moderately, long love doth so;
15   Too swift arrives as tardy as too slow.

              Enter JULIET.

    Here comes the lady. O, so light a foot
    Will ne'er wear out the everlasting flint;
    A lover may bestride the gossamers
    That idles in the wanton summer air,
20   And yet not fall, so light is vanity.

JULIET Good even to my ghostly confessor.

FRIAR LAWRENCE Romeo shall thank thee, daughter, for us both.

         [ROMEO *kisses* JULIET.]

That after ... not that the future will not punish us with unhappiness
countervail ... joy counterbalance possible grief in future

powder gunpowder
as they kiss when they come into contact
Is loathsome ... deliciousness may turn out to taste so badly because it is so delicious
confounds ruins, destroys
Too swift ... slow overhastiness is as bad as too much hesitation

O, so ... flint Juliet moves so lightly that she will not wear out the cobblestones in the street over which she may walk
A lover ... gossamers a lover may ride on a spider's web
idles floats idly
so light ... vanity such is the trivial pursuit of love

'Sweeten with thy breath
this neighbour air'
(dir. Baz Luhrmann, 1996)

As much ... too much I must
repay my thanks to him;
otherwise I will be in his debt

Be heaped ... be more is piled up
like my great pleasure and if you
are more skilful than I am
To blazon to celebrate; proclaim

This neighbour ... tongue the air
about us and let the music of
your voice
either each other

Conceit ... ornament understanding is much more
important than words idly
spoken
They are ... worth only love's
beggars can count their wealth
I cannot ... wealth I cannot total
up the full amount of my love
(for Romeo)
by your leaves with your
permission
incorporate ... one unites you in
holy matrimony

JULIET As much to him, else is his thanks too much.

[JULIET *returns his kiss.*]

ROMEO Ah, Juliet, if the measure of thy joy
      Be heaped like mine, and that thy skill be more   25
      To blazon it, then sweeten with thy breath

      This neighbour air, and let rich music's tongue
      Unfold the imagined happiness that both
      Receive in either by this dear encounter.

JULIET Conceit, more rich in matter than in words,   30
      Brags of his substance, not of ornament;
      They are but beggars that can count their worth,
      But my true love is grown to such excess
      I cannot sum up sum of half my wealth.

FRIAR LAWRENCE Come, come with me, and we will make short   35
      work,
      For by your leaves, you shall not stay alone
      Till Holy Church incorporate two in one.

[*Exeunt*]

Activities

1. Compare Text 8 with Text 6, describing resemblances and differences.

2. Analyse the language of the three characters in chronological order, putting special emphasis on the images they use.

Act 3

Act 3 – Scene 1

9

Tybalt, still angry that Romeo has sneaked into the ball, looks for Romeo in the marketplace. At first only Benvolio and Mercutio are there, but then the newly-wed Romeo appears and is challenged by Tybalt. Mercutio steps in to defend Romeo and a fight begins. In the course of this duel, Tybalt (perhaps accidentally) kills Mercutio. In order to avenge his friend, Romeo kills Tybalt in return.

Enter PRINCE, *old* MONTAGUE, CAPULET, *their* WIVES, *and all.*

PRINCE Where are the vile beginners of this fray?

BENVOLIO O noble Prince, I can discover all
    The unlucky manage of this fatal brawl;
    There lies the man, slain by young Romeo,
5   That slew thy kinsman, brave Mercutio.

LADY CAPULET Tybalt, my cousin! O my brother's child!
    O Prince! O husband! O, the blood is spilled
    Of my dear kinsman. Prince, as thou art true,
    For blood of ours, shed blood of Montague.
10 O cousin, cousin!

PRINCE Benvolio, who began this bloody fray?

BENVOLIO Tybalt, here slain, whom Romeo's hand did slay.
    Romeo, that spoke him fair, bid him bethink
    How nice the quarrel was, and urged withal
15 Your high displeasure; all this, utterèd
    With gentle breath, calm look, knees humbly bowed,
    Could not take truce with the unruly spleen
    Of Tybalt deaf to peace, but that he tilts
    With piercing steel at bold Mercutio's breast,
20 Who, all as hot, turns deadly point to point,
    And with a martial scorn, with one hand beats
    Cold death aside, and with the other sends
    It back to Tybalt, whose dexterity
    Retorts it. Romeo he cries aloud,
25 'Hold, friends! friends, part!' and swifter than his tongue,
    His agile arm beats down their fatal points,
    And 'twixt them rushes; underneath whose arm
    An envious thrust from Tybalt hit the life
    Of stout Mercutio, and then Tybalt fled;
30 But by and by comes back to Romeo,

discover reveal
manage course

spoke him fair spoke very kindly to him
bethink consider
nice trivial
urged ... displeasure mentioned your disgust of all civil strife
take truce make peace
unruly spleen furious rage

all as hot as angry as Tybalt
martial scorn warlike contempt (of each other)
Cold death the sheath of the dagger
dexterity skill
Retorts returns

'twixt between

Who had but newly entertained revenge,
And to't they go like lightning, for, ere I
Could draw to part them, was stout Tybalt slain;
And as he fell, did Romeo turn and fly.
This is the truth, or let Benvolio die.   35

LADY CAPULET   He is a kinsman to the Montague,
Affection makes him false, he speaks not true:
Some twenty of them fought in this black strife,
And all those twenty could but kill one life.
I beg for justice, which thou, Prince, must give: 40
Romeo slew Tybalt, Romeo must not live.

PRINCE   Romeo slew him, he slew Mercutio;
Who now the price of his dear blood doth owe?

MONTAGUE   Not Romeo, Prince, he was Mercutio's friend;
His fault concludes but what the law should end,   45
The life of Tybalt.

PRINCE   And for that offence
Immediately we do exile him hence.
I have an interest in your hearts' proceeding:
My blood for your rude brawls doth lie a-bleeding;
But I'll amerce you with so strong a fine   50
That you shall all repent the loss of mine.
I will be deaf to pleading and excuses,
Nor tears nor prayers shall purchase out abuses:
Therefore use none. Let Romeo hence in haste,
Else, when he is found, that hour is his last.   55
Bear hence this body, and attend our will:
Mercy but murders, pardoning those that kill.

Exeunt

but ... entertained just considered

fly flee

Affection ... false he is a liar out of friendship for Romeo

Who now ... owe who is responsible for Mercutio's death?
concludes but only finishes
should end would have done

I have ... proceeding I am personally involved in your feud
My blood my kinsman
amerce punish
mine my relative

purchase out abuses soften my heart

attend strictly obey
Mercy ... kill mercy will only lead to new murders if I pardon anybody

'Tybalt deaf to peace'
(dir. Franco Zeffirelli, 1968)

Activities

1. Describe the different functions of each speaker in this open-air trial scene.

2. Do you consider Benvolio's speech to be a neutral testimony, a defence of his friend Romeo, or primarily a lively report? Find arguments for or against these different views.

3. Watch chapter 20 from 0:59:50. In the play, Tybalt challenges Romeo because he wants to protect his honour and reputation. Which aspect of the duel is highlighted in the film?

4. Towards the end of the scene, what imagery is used to signal approaching disaster?

Act 3 – Scene 2

10

JULIET Ay me, what news? Why dost thou wring thy hands?

NURSE Ah weraday, he's dead, he's dead, he's dead!
We are undone, lady, we are undone.
Alack the day, he's gone, he's killed, he's dead!

5 JULIET Can heaven be so envious?

NURSE   Romeo can,
Though heaven cannot. O Romeo, Romeo!
Who ever would have thought it? Romeo!

JULIET What devil art thou that dost torment me thus?
This torture should be roared in dismal hell.
10 Hath Romeo slain himself? Say thou but 'ay',
And that bare vowel 'I' shall poison more
Than the death-darting eye of cockatrice.
I am not I, if there be such an 'ay',
Or those eyes shut, that makes thee answer 'ay'.
15 If he be slain, say 'ay', or if not, 'no':
Brief sounds determine my weal or woe.

NURSE I saw the wound, I saw it with mine eyes
(God save the mark!), here on his manly breast:
A piteous corse, a bloody piteous corse,
20 Pale, pale as ashes, all bedaubed in blood,
All in gore blood; I sounded at the sight.

JULIET O break, my heart, poor bankrout, break at once!
To prison, eyes, ne'er look on liberty!
Vile earth, to earth resign, end motion here,
25 And thou and Romeo press one heavy bier!

weraday what a day
undone ruined

envious cruel

Romeo can (be so cruel)

dismal evil

cockatrice a creature with a serpent's body and a cock's head; looking in its eyes was thought to be fatal

Brief … woe a short answer will make me happy or sad

God … mark may God forgive me for telling you such horrible news
corse corpse, dead body
bedaubed covered
gore clotted, thick
sounded fainted
poor bankrout I have lost everything if Romeo is dead
Vile … resign sink into the grave, my body!
press … bier lie in one grave

NURSE O Tybalt, Tybalt, the best friend I had!
    O courteous Tybalt, honest gentleman,
    That ever I should live to see thee dead!

JULIET What storm is this that blows so contrary?
    Is Romeo slaughtered? and is Tybalt dead?   30
    My dearest cousin, and my dearer lord?
    Then, dreadful trumpet, sound the general doom,
    For who is living, if those two are gone?

NURSE Tybalt is gone and Romeo banishèd,
    Romeo that killed him, he is banishèd.   35

JULIET O God, did Romeo's hand shed Tybalt's blood?

NURSE It did, it did, alas the day, it did!

JULIET O serpent heart, hid with a flow'ring face!
    Did ever dragon keep so fair a cave?
    Beautiful tyrant, fiend angelical!   40
    Dove-feathered raven, wolvish-ravening lamb!
    Despisèd substance of divinest show!
    Just opposite to what thou justly seem'st,
    A damnèd saint, an honourable villain!
    O nature, what hadst thou to do in hell   45
    When thou didst bower the spirit of a fiend
    In mortal paradise of such sweet flesh?
    Was ever book containing such vile matter
    So fairly bound? O that deceit should dwell
    In such a gorgeous palace!   50

NURSE   There's no trust,
    No faith, no honesty in men, all perjured,
    All forsworn, all naught, all dissemblers.
    Ah, where's my man? Give me some aqua-vitae;
    These griefs, these woes, these sorrows make me old.
    Shame come to Romeo!   55

contrary first in one direction then in the other

general doom the end of everything

O serpent ... face devil's heart that hides behind a kind face
keep ... cave so guard its treasure
fiend cruel person
Despised ... show brutal reality with angelic face

bower enclose, cover

gorgeous palace extremely beautiful body

perjured oath-breakers
forsworn liars
naught wicked
dissemblers deceivers
aqua vitae brandy

'O God, did Romeo's hand shed Tybalt's blood?' (dir. Franco Zeffirelli, 1968)

JULIET   Blistered be thy tongue
    For such a wish! he was not born to shame:
    Upon his brow shame is ashamed to sit;
    For 'tis a throne where honour may be crowned
    Sole monarch of the universal earth.
60 O what a beast was I to chide at him!

NURSE Will you speak well of him that killed your cousin?

JULIET Shall I speak ill of him that is my husband?
    Ah, poor my lord, what tongue shall smooth thy name,
    When I, thy three-hours wife, have mangled it?
65 But wherefore, villain, didst thou kill my cousin?
    That villain cousin would have killed my husband.
    Back, foolish tears, back to your native spring,
    Your tributary drops belong to woe,
    Which you mistaking offer up to joy.
70 My husband lives that Tybalt would have slain,
    And Tybalt's dead that would have slain my husband:
    All this is comfort, wherefore weep I then?
    Some word there was, worser than Tybalt's death,
    That murdered me; I would forget it fain,
75 But O, it presses to my memory,
    Like damnèd guilty deeds to sinners' minds:
    'Tybalt is dead, and Romeo banishèd.'
    That 'banishèd', that one word 'banishèd',
    Hath slain ten thousand Tybalts. Tybalt's death
80 Was woe enough if it had ended there;
    Or if sour woe delights in fellowship,
    And needly will be ranked with other griefs,
    Why followed not, when she said 'Tybalt's dead',
    'Thy father' or 'thy mother', nay, or both,
85 Which modern lamentation might have moved?
    But with a rear-ward following Tybalt's death,
    'Romeo is banishèd': to speak that word,
    Is father, mother, Tybalt, Romeo, Juliet,
    All slain, all dead. 'Romeo is banishèd!'
90 There is no end, no limit, measure, bound,
    In that word's death, no words can that woe sound.
    Where is my father and my mother, Nurse?

NURSE Weeping and wailing over Tybalt's corse.
    Will you go to them? I will bring you thither.

95 JULIET Wash they his wounds with tears? mine shall be spent,
    When theirs are dry, for Romeo's banishment.
    Take up those cords. Poor ropes, you are beguiled,
    Both you and I, for Romeo is exiled.
    He made you for a highway to my bed,
100 But I, a maid, die maiden-widowèd.

---

bom to shame born to feel ashamed
Upon ... sit he would feel uncomfortable to have done something shameful
For ... earth he is a highly honourable person
chide at speak ill of

smooth purify, clear
mangled spoil, wounded

Back ... spring back from where you come

Your tributary ... joy you are not tears of grief but of joy

worser worse
fain happily

presses ... minds is in my memory like cruel deeds in the minds of sinners

sour woe bitter distress
fellowship company
needly will be ranked has to be compared
followed not why did she not add that also father and mother were dead?
Which ... moved this news might have been lamented
rear-ward rearguard (an attack from behind)

no words ... sound no words can describe that grief

you are beguiled you have been cheated

for a highway find a way
maiden-widowèd a widow without having been a wife

After this conversation, the nurse leaves and promises to find Romeo in order to bring him to Juliet.

Activities

1. Find and describe resemblances between Texts 7 and 10.

2. Point out differences between the two texts in question.

3. During the present encounter with her nurse, Juliet exhibits a whole range of conflicting emotions. Give examples and explain them in chronological order.

Act 3 – Scenes 3 and 4

After his banishment, Romeo is desperate and seeks the advice of Friar Lawrence. The idea of a life outside Verona, without Juliet, is so terrible that he even tries to kill himself. The friar advises Romeo to go into exile in Mantua and wait there until all the problems have been solved. In the meantime, Capulet, who still has no idea about his daughter's secret marriage, decides that Juliet should be married to Paris the following Thursday.

Act 3 – Scene 5
Juliet's bedroom

11

Enter ROMEO *and* JULIET *aloft at the window.*

JULIET Wilt thou be gone? It is not yet near day:
   It was the nightingale, and not the lark,
   That pierced the fearful hollow of thine ear;
   Nightly she sings on yond pomegranate tree.
   Believe me, love, it was the nightingale.   5

ROMEO It was the lark, the herald of the morn,
   No nightingale. Look, love, what envious streaks
   Do lace the severing clouds in yonder east:
   Night's candles are burnt out, and jocund day
   Stands tiptoe on the misty mountain tops.   10
   I must be gone and live, or stay and die.

JULIET Yond light is not daylight, I know it, I:
   It is some meteor that the sun exhaled

Glossary (left margin):

lark this bird was said to announce daybreak
fearful timorous

envious jealous, malicious
Do lace ... clouds pierce through the separating clouds
jocund cheerful

live stay alive

exhaled produced

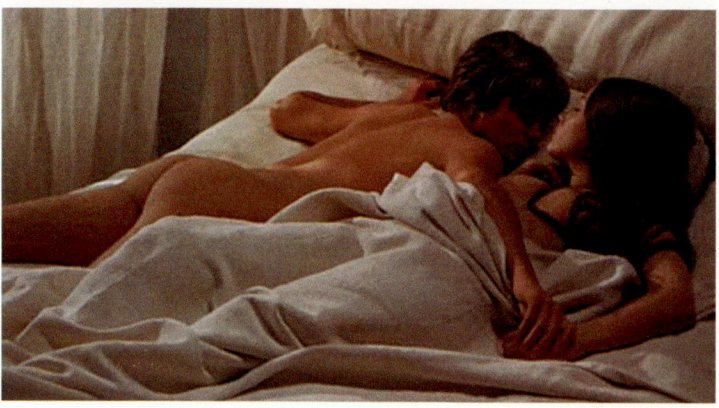

'I have more care to stay
than will to go'
(dir. Franco Zeffirelli, 1968)

To be to thee this night a torch-bearer,
15 And light thee on thy way to Mantua.
Therefore stay yet, thou need'st not to be gone.

ROMEO Let me be tane, let me be put to death,
I am content, so thou wilt have it so.
I'll say yon grey is not the morning's eye,
20 'Tis but the pale reflex of Cynthia's brow;
Nor that is not the lark whose notes do beat
The vaulty heaven so high above our heads.
I have more care to stay than will to go:
Come, death, and welcome! Juliet wills it so.
25 How is't, my soul? Let's talk, it is not day.

JULIET It is, it is, hie hence, be gone, away!
It is the lark that sings so out of tune,
Straining harsh discords and unpleasing sharps.
Some say the lark makes sweet division:
30 This doth not so, for she divideth us.
Some say the lark and loathèd toad changed eyes;
O now I would they had changed voices too,
Since arm from arm that voice doth us affray,
Hunting thee hence with hunt's-up to the day.
35 O now be gone, more light and light it grows.

ROMEO More light and light, more dark and dark our woes!

Enter NURSE *hastily.*

NURSE Madam!

JULIET Nurse?

NURSE Your lady mother is coming to your chamber.
40 The day is broke, be wary, look about.   *Exit*

JULIET Then, window, let day in, and let life out.

ROMEO Farewell, farewell! one kiss, and I'll descend.

He goeth down.

tane caught, captured

reflex reflection
Cynthia's brow the moon
vaulty heaven sky

care desire, wish

hie hence off you go

Straining ... sharps with its
strong discords and shrill notes
division melody
This the lark
loathèd ... eyes toads were
supposed to have more
beautiful eyes than larks
would wish
Since arm ... day the lark
separates us and chases you
away with a huntsman's early
morning call
More light ... our woes much
lighter our joys, much darker
our sorrows

is broke has begun

ay eternal
friend lover

O, by ... years if I count this way
I'll be much older

discourses conversations

ill-divining pessimistic
low under my window

Dry ... blood too much grief was
supposed to drink up blood,
thus making the face look pale
fickle unreliable
dost thou are you doing
That ... faith who is known to be
steadfast

JULIET Art thou gone so, love, lord, ay husband, friend?
    I must hear from thee every day in the hour,
    For in a minute there are many days.   45
    O, by this count I shall be much in years
    Ere I again behold my Romeo!

ROMEO [*From below*] Farewell!
    I will omit no opportunity
    That may convey my greetings, love, to thee.   50

JULIET O think'st thou we shall ever meet again?

ROMEO I doubt it not, and all these woes shall serve
    For sweet discourses in our times to come.

JULIET O God, I have an ill-divining soul!
    Methinks I see thee now, thou art so low,   55
    As one dead in the bottom of a tomb.
    Either my eyesight fails, or thou look'st pale.

ROMEO And trust me, love, in my eye so do you:
    Dry sorrow drinks our blood. Adieu, adieu!   *Exit*

JULIET O Fortune, Fortune, all men call thee fickle;   60
    If thou art fickle, what dost thou with him
    That is renowned for faith? Be fickle, Fortune:
    For then I hope thou wilt not keep him long,
    But send him back.

Lady Capulet tells Juliet that she will be married to Paris soon, but Juliet refuses. When Lord Capulet gets to know this, he threatens to banish her from the family. Afterwards Juliet is comforted by the nurse, who advises her to marry Paris because he would be a better husband than Romeo. Juliet decides to seek Friar Lawrence's help.

Activities

1. This heart-breaking parting scene is renowned for its metaphors and personifications. Elaborate on this.

2. To what extent do the two lovers influence and persuade each other?

3. Some aspects of the dialogue seem rather unexpected, even paradoxical*. Point them out.

4. Watch chapter 22 from 01:15:50 – end. How does this scene contrast with the previous extract you have seen? What colour imagery is used here and to what effect?

5. How does the camera capture Juliet's premonition about approaching death towards the end of the scene? How does it suggest that disaster might strike?

Act 4

Act 4 – Scene 1
Friar Lawrence's cell

12

Enter FRIAR LAWRENCE *and* COUNTY PARIS.

FRIAR LAWRENCE On Thursday, sir? the time is very short.

PARIS My father Capulet will have it so,
  And I am nothing slow to slack his haste.

FRIAR LAWRENCE You say you do not know the lady's mind?
5   Uneven is the course, I like it not.

PARIS Immoderately she weeps for Tybalt's death,
  And therefore have I little talked of love,
  For Venus smiles not in a house of tears.
  Now, sir, her father counts it dangerous
10   That she do give her sorrow so much sway;
  And in his wisdom hastes our marriage
  To stop the inundation of her tears,
  Which too much minded by herself alone
  May be put from her by society.
15   Now do you know the reason of this haste.

FRIAR LAWRENCE [*Aside*] I would I knew not why it should be
  slowed. –
  Look, sir, here comes the lady toward my cell.

Enter JULIET.

PARIS Happily met, my lady and my wife!

JULIET That may be, sir, when I may be a wife.

20 PARIS That 'may be' must be, love, on Thursday next.

JULIET What must be shall be.

FRIAR LAWRENCE   That's a certain text.

PARIS Come you to make confession to this father?

JULIET To answer that, I should confess to you.

PARIS Do not deny to him that you love me.

25 JULIET I will confess to you that I love him.

PARIS So will ye, I am sure, that you love me.

JULIET If I do so, it will be of more price,
  Being spoke behind your back, than to your face.

PARIS Poor soul, thy face is much abused with tears.

---

father father-in-law
And I … haste and I certainly won't stop him acting quickly

Uneven … course acting so quickly is rather unusual
immoderately excessively

For Venus … tears love is not a good companion of sadness
counts considers
do give … sway gives in to her sorrow

too much … alone brooding too much upon her grief alone
May be … society may change in other people's company

I would … slowed I had better not know why it should be postponed

That's a certain text that is truly said

So will ye you will also tell him

of more … face worthier being spoken behind your back than into your face
abused spoiled

spite damage

Juliet The tears have got small victory by that,   30
    For it was bad enough before their spite.

Paris Thou wrong'st it more than tears with that report.

I spake ... face I said to my face (i.e. openly)

Juliet That is no slander, sir, which is a truth,
    And what I spake, I spake it to my face.

Paris Thy face is mine, and thou hast slandered it.   35

Are ... leisure can you spare me a minute

Juliet It may be so, for it is not mine own.
    Are you at leisure, holy father, now,
    Or shall I come to you at evening mass?

My ... me it is convenient for me
entreat ... alone ask you to leave us
shield forbid that
rouse ye wake you up

Friar Lawrence My leisure serves me, pensive daughter, now.
    My lord, we must entreat the time alone.   40

Paris God shield I should disturb devotion!
    Juliet, on Thursday early will I rouse ye;
    Till then adieu, and keep this holy kiss.   *Exit*

After Paris has left, the friar comes up with a risky plan to solve Juliet's dilemma. He offers her a sleeping potion that will make her appear dead. He advises her to drink this the night before the planned wedding so that her family believes her dead and buries her. Romeo, he promises her, will rescue her from the tomb and take her to Mantua with him.

Activities

1. Characterize the behaviour of County Paris, Friar Lawrence, and Juliet in the present passage.

2. Would you consider this passage predominantly serious or comic? Find arguments for both views.

3. Have a look at this still, taken from chapter 23 of the DVD (dir. Baz Luhrmann, 1996). How would you characterize Dave Paris? What role does costume play to establish the relationship between him and Juliet?

Act 4 – Scene 2

Capulet's mansion

13

Enter Father CAPULET, *Mother* LADY CAPULET, NURSE,
and SERVINGMEN, *two or three.*

CAPULET So many guests invite as here are writ.

Exit SERVINGMAN

Sirrah, go hire me twenty cunning cooks.

cunning skilled

SERVINGMAN You shall have none ill, sir, for I'll try if they can lick
their fingers.

none ill experienced cooks
try make a test
lick ... fingers taste what they
have cooked

5 CAPULET How canst thou try them so?

SERVINGMAN Marry, sir, 'tis an ill cook that cannot lick his own
fingers; therefore he that cannot lick his fingers goes not with
me.

ill bad

CAPULET Go, be gone.

Exit SERVINGMAN

10   We shall be much unfurnished for this time.
What, is my daughter gone to Friar Lawrence?

much unfurnished fully
unprepared (for the wedding)

NURSE Ay forsooth.

Ay, forsooth she did, indeed

CAPULET Well, he may chance to do some good on her.
A peevish self-willed harlotry it is.

A peevish ... it is she is a
stubborn self-centred little fool

Enter JULIET.

15 NURSE See where she comes from shrift with merry look.

shrift confession

CAPULET How now, my headstrong, where have you been gadding?

gadding running around

'How now, my headstrong,
where have you been gadding?'
(dir. Franco Zeffirelli, 1968)

behests instructions
enjoined asked, demanded

JULIET Where I have learnt me to repent the sin
    Of disobedient opposition
    To you and your behests, and am enjoined
    By holy Lawrence to fall prostrate here   20
    To beg your pardon.

                           She kneels down.

               Pardon, I beseech you!
    Henceforward I am ever ruled by you.

knot knit up marriage bond
fixed until

CAPULET Send for the County, go tell him of this.
    I'll have this knot knit up tomorrow morning.

becomèd decent, proper

JULIET I met the youthful lord at Lawrence' cell,   25
    And gave him what becomèd love I might,
    Not stepping o'er the bounds of modesty.

bound indebted

CAPULET Why, I am glad on't, this is well, stand up.
    This is as't should be. Let me see the County;
    Ay, marry, go, I say, and fetch him hither.   30
    Now afore God, this reverend holy Friar,
    All our whole city is much bound to him.

closet room
sort choose
needful necessary
to furnish me for me to put on

JULIET Nurse, will you go with me into my closet,
    To help me sort such needful ornaments
    As you think fit to furnish me tomorrow?   35

LADY CAPULET No, not till Thursday, there is time enough.

CAPULET Go, Nurse, go with her, we'll to church tomorrow.

                Exeunt JULIET *and* NURSE

We shall ... provision we do not
have everything we need for the
wedding
stir about get busy
warrant assure
deck up her get her dressed
as a bride
let me alone let me do it my way
They ... forth the servants are
doing their job
prepare ... against tell him what
will happen
My ... light I am really so happy
Since because
so reclaimed brought to her
senses

LADY CAPULET We shall be short in our provision,
    'Tis now near night.

CAPULET   Tush, I will stir about,
    And all things shall be well, I warrant thee, wife: 40
    Go thou to Juliet, help to deck up her;
    I'll not to bed tonight; let me alone,
    I'll play the huswife for this once. What ho!
    They are all forth. Well, I will walk myself
    To County Paris, to prepare up him   45
    Against tomorrow. My heart is wondrous light,
    Since this same wayward girl is so reclaimed.

                              Exeunt

Activities

1. This scene contains various elements of comic relief within the action of the tragedy. Explain them.

2. In how far does Juliet's behaviour differ here in comparison with previous passages, and what do you think of this?

Act 4 – Scene 3
Juliet's bedroom

14

JULIET I have a faint cold fear thrills through my veins
    That almost freezes up the heat of life:
    I'll call them back again to comfort me.
    Nurse! – What should she do here?
5   My dismal scene I needs must act alone.
    Come, vial.
    What if this mixture do not work at all?
    Shall I be married then tomorrow morning?
    No, no, this shall forbid it; lie thou there.

              Laying down her dagger.

10   What if it be a poison which the Friar
    Subtly hath ministered to have me dead,
    Lest in this marriage he should be dishonoured,
    Because he married me before to Romeo?
    I fear it is, and yet methinks it should not,
15   For he hath still been tried a holy man.
    How if, when I am laid into the tomb,
    I wake before the time that Romeo
    Come to redeem me? There's a fearful point!
    Shall I not then be stifled in the vault,
20   To whose foul mouth no healthsome air breathes in,
    And there die strangled ere my Romeo comes?
    Or if I live, is it not very like
    The horrible conceit of death and night,
    Together with the terror of the place –
25   As in a vault, an ancient receptacle,
    Where for this many hundred years the bones
    Of all my buried ancestors are packed,

thrills that runs

My dismal ... alone I have to solve this desperate situation myself

subtly cunningly
ministered given me

hath still ... tried is still regarded
How if what happens
I wake and wake up
redeem save
stifled suffocated
To whose ... in which hardly ever gets fresh air
strangled of suffocation

conceit thought

As in ... receptacle as if being in a vaulted old tomb

'I have a faint cold fear thrills through my veins'
(dir. Baz Luhrmann, 1996)

Where bloody Tybalt, yet but green in earth,
Lies fest'ring in his shroud, where, as they say,
At some houts in the night spirits resort –   30
Alack, alack, is it not like that I,
So early waking – what with loathsome smells,
And shrieks like mandrakes' torn out of the earth,
That living mortals hearing them run mad –
O, if I wake, shall I not be distraught,   35
Environèd with all these hideous fears,
And madly play with my forefathers' joints,
And pluck the mangled Tybalt from his shroud,
And in this rage, with some great kinsman's bone,
As with a club, dash out my desp'rate brains?   40
O look! methinks I see my cousin's ghost
Seeking out Romeo that did spit his body
Upon a rapier's point. Stay, Tybalt, stay!
Romeo, Romeo, Romeo! Here's drink – I drink to thee.

She falls upon her bed, within the curtains.

yet but ... earth recently laid to rest

resort meet

shrieks ... earth shrieks that mandrakes make when pulled up by the root
distraught mad
environed with surrounded by
joints bones
pluck ... shroud pull away the shroud in which Tybalt is wrapped up
rage madness
dash kick

did spit ran a sword through

Activities

1. Check the term 'dilemma' in the glossary and give a short description of Juliet's present situation.

2. By what fears and visions is Juliet haunted, and how does she try to overcome them?

3. Watch chapter 25 until 01:27:33. How does the director convey Juliet's fear? How does the cinematography* indicate that the friar's plan might go wrong?

Act 4 – Scene 4

The day of Juliet's and Paris's wedding has come. Capulet supervises the preparations and tells the nurse to wake up Juliet.

Act 5

Act 5 – Scenes 1 and 2

> When entering Juliet's chamber, the nurse finds Juliet's lifeless body and obviously thinks she is dead. The entire family is shocked and starts mourning the loss of their daughter. From now on, the events escalate quickly. Romeo is misinformed that Juliet has died, so he decides to return to Verona and die with her. He looks for an appropriate weapon to kill himself and buys a bottle of poison from an apothecary. Meanwhile, the Friar learns that Romeo has not received his letter about the plan to fake Juliet's death. Worried that everything might go horribly wrong, he decides to take Juliet's body into his cell and wait for Romeo's arrival.

Act 5 – Scene 3

15

> Romeo has returned to Verona in order to mourn the presumably dead Juliet. He wants to visit her tomb alone and commit suicide next to her body. But he is not alone because Paris has also come to pay his bride a last visit.

PARIS This is that banished haughty Montague,
    That murdered my love's cousin, with which grief
    It is supposèd the fair creature died,
    And here is come to do some villainous shame
5   To the dead bodies. I will apprehend him.

               [*Steps forth.*]

    Stop thy unhallowed toil, vile Montague!
    Can vengeance be pursued further than death?
    Condemnèd villain, I do apprehend thee.
    Obey and go with me, for thou must die.

10 ROMEO I must indeed, and therefore came I hither.
    Good gentle youth, tempt not a desp'rate man,
    Fly hence and leave me. Think upon these gone,
    Let them affright thee. I beseech thee, youth,
    Put not another sin upon my head,
15   By urging me to fury: O be gone!
    By heaven, I love thee better than myself,
    For I come hither armed against myself.
    Stay not, be gone; live, and hereafter say,
    A madman's mercy bid thee run away.

20 PARIS I do defy thy conjuration,
    And apprehend thee for a felon here.

---

with which grief and because of grieving Tybalt's death

do some … To dismember
apprehend him prevent him from doing anything shameful

unhallowed toil unholy doing

apprehend arrest

these gone those people buried here
affright thee scare you away

armed against ready to do harm to

defy thy conjuration ignore what you say
for a felon as a criminal

'For here lies Juliet, and her beauty makes this vault a feasting presence full of light' (dir. Baz Luhrmann, 1996)

have at thee draw your sword

ROMEO Wilt thou provoke me? then have at thee, boy!

[*They fight.*]

PAGE O Lord, they fight! I will go call the Watch.   [*Exit*]

PARIS O, I am slain! [*Falls.*] If thou be merciful,
Open the tomb, lay me with Juliet. [*Dies.*]   25

peruse have a close look at

betossèd soul mind full of other problems
attend listen to

ROMEO In faith, I will. Let me peruse this face.
Mercutio's kinsman, noble County Paris!
What said my man, when my betossèd soul
Did not attend him as we rode? I think
He told me Paris should have married Juliet.   30
Said he not so? or did I dream it so?
Or am I mad, hearing him talk of Juliet,
To think it was so? O give me thy hand,

One writ ... book you that will be my misfortune's fellow
triumphant pompous, great
lantern it will be an illumination

One writ with me in sour misfortune's book!
I'll bury thee in a triumphant grave.   35
A grave? O no, a lantern, slaughtered youth;
For here lies Juliet, and her beauty makes

a feasting presence look like a chamber
Death i.e. Paris
dead man i.e. Romeo

This vault a feasting presence full of light.
Death, lie thou there, by a dead man interred.

[*Laying* PARIS *in the tomb.*]

keepers nurses
lightning raising of human spirits

How oft when men are at the point of death   40
Have they been merry, which their keepers call
A light'ning before death! O how may I
Call this a light'ning? O my love, my wife,
Death, that hath sucked the honey of thy breath,
Hath had no power yet upon thy beauty: 45

beauty's ensign the sign of your beauty

is not ... there cannot be seen
bloody death

Thou art not conquered, beauty's ensign yet
Is crimson in thy lips and in thy cheeks,
And Death's pale flag is not advancèd there.
Tybalt, liest thou there in thy bloody sheet?
O, what more favour can I do to thee   50

twain two parts
To sunder his to get rid of my own life

Than with that hand that cut thy youth in twain
To sunder his that was thine enemy?
Forgive me, cousin. Ah, dear Juliet,

'Here's to my love!'
(dir. Franco Zeffirelli, 1968)

Why art thou yet so fair? Shall I believe
55   That unsubstantial Death is amorous,
And that the lean abhorrèd monster keeps
Thee here in dark to be his paramour?
For fear of that, I still will stay with thee,
And never from this palace of dim night
60   Depart again. Here, here will I remain
With worms that are thy chambermaids; O here
Will I set up my everlasting rest,
And shake the yoke of inauspicious stars
From this world-wearied flesh. Eyes, look your last!
65   Arms, take your last embrace! and, lips, O you
The doors of breath, seal with a righteous kiss
A dateless bargain to engrossing Death!
Come, bitter conduct, come, unsavoury guide!
Thou desperate pilot, now at once run on
70   The dashing rocks thy seasick weary bark!
Here's to my love! [*Drinks.*] O true apothecary!
Thy drugs are quick. Thus with a kiss I die. [*Dies.*]

unsubstantial death having no body
abhorrèd horrible
paramour beloved, mistress
still will will forever
palace resting place

the yoke ... stars off the burden of life laid upon me by misfortune

A dateless ... Death a bargain for eternity as death wins everything
conduct escort
unsavoury guide bitter-tasting poison
now at once ... bark who has steered his ship onto the fatal rocks

Activities

1. Describe the atmosphere evoked by this passage before and after the death of Paris.

2. Point out some differences between Romeo's last words and Juliet's preceding soliloquy (Text 14).

3. Watch chapter 27 from 01:38:05 – 01:39:28. How does this setting compare to the tomb in the play?

4. Continue watching this chapter until the end. As you will see, Luhrmann makes a significant change to Romeo and Juliet's suicide scene. What exactly does he change and what effect does this create?

5. What do we see after Juliet has shot herself? What are the implications?

16

FRIAR LAWRENCE Romeo!

Friar stoops and looks on the blood and weapons.

Alack, alack, what blood is this which stains
The stony entrance of this sepulchre?
What mean these masterless and gory swords
To lie discoloured by this place of peace?   5

Enters the tomb.

Romeo! O, pale! Who else? What, Paris too?
And steeped in blood? Ah, what an unkind hour
Is guilty of this lamentable chance!

JULIET rises.

The lady stirs.

JULIET O comfortable Friar, where is my lord?   10
I do remember well where I should be;
And there I am. Where is my Romeo?

Noise within.

FRIAR LAWRENCE I hear some noise, lady. Come from that nest
Of death, contagion, and unnatural sleep.
A greater power than we can contradict   15
Hath thwarted our intents. Come, come away.
Thy husband in thy bosom there lies dead;
And Paris too. Come, I'll dispose of thee
Among a sisterhood of holy nuns.
Stay not to question, for the Watch is coming.   20
Come go, good Juliet, I dare no longer stay.   *Exit*

sepulchre tomb

What mean ... discoloured who do these bloody sword belong to which lie here stained with blood

steeped covered
what an ... chance what inhuman time is responsible for this terrible event

comfortable kind and gentle

contagion disease, poison
unnatural caused by my drug

than we ... intents which we are unable to oppose has ruined our plans

dispose ... among bring you to

'O happy dagger'
(dir. Franco Zeffirelli, 1968)

JULIET Go get thee hence, for I will not away.
What's here? a cup closed in my true love's hand?
Poison I see hath been his timeless end.

25 O churl, drunk all, and left no friendly drop
To help me after? I will kiss thy lips,
Haply some poison yet doth hang on them,
To make me die with a restorative.
Thy lips are warm.

30 CAPTAIN OF THE WATCH [*Within*] Lead, boy, which way?

JULIET Yea, noise? Then I'll be brief. O happy dagger,

Taking Romeo's dagger.

This is thy sheath;

Stabs herself.

there rust, and let me die.

Falls on Romeo's body and dies.

timeless untimely	
churl thoughtless man	
Haply perhaps	
make ... restorative let me die with the help of this 'medicine'	
This my bosom	
rust remain forever	

After Juliet has stabbed herself, several characters enter the tomb with torches. They are shocked to find the three bodies and try to find out what has happened.

Activities

1. Comment on the considerable number of explicit and implicit stage-directions in this short passage.

2. How do Juliet's final speeches compare with the preceding soliloquies (Texts 14 and 15)?

17

CAPULET and LADY CAPULET enter the tomb.

CAPULET O heavens! O wife, look how our daughter bleeds!
This dagger hath mistane, for lo his house
Is empty on the back of Montague,
And it mis-sheathèd in my daughter's bosom!

5 LADY CAPULET O me, this sight of death is as a bell
That warns my old age to a sepulchre.

They return from the tomb.

Enter MONTAGUE.

mistane killed the wrong person	
his house ... Montague its sheath should be in Montague's back	
And but	
warns ... sepulchre summons me to my grave	

PRINCE Come, Montague, for thou art early up
  To see thy son and heir now early down.

MONTAGUE Alas, my liege, my wife is dead tonight;
  Grief of my son's exile hath stopped her breath.   10
  What further woe conspires against mine age?

PRINCE Look and thou shalt see.

Montague enters the tomb and returns.

MONTAGUE O thou untaught! what manners is in this,
  To press before thy father to a grave?

PRINCE Seal up the mouth of outrage for a while,   15
  Till we can clear these ambiguities,
  And know their spring, their head, their true descent,
  And then will I be general of your woes,
  And lead you even to death. Mean time forbear,
  And let mischance be slave to patience.   20
  Bring forth the parties of suspicion.

FRIAR LAWRENCE I am the greatest, able to do least,
  Yet most suspected, as the time and place
  Doth make against me, of this direful murder;
  And here I stand both to impeach and purge   25
  Myself condemnèd and myself excused.

PRINCE Then say at once what thou dost know in this.

FRIAR LAWRENCE I will be brief, for my short date of breath
  Is not so long as is a tedious tale.
  Romeo, there dead, was husband to that Juliet,   30
  And she, there dead, that Romeo's faithful wife:
  I married them, and their stol'n marriage day
  Was Tybalt's doomsday, whose untimely death
  Banished the new-made bridegroom from this city,

  For whom, and not for Tybalt, Juliet pined.   35
  You, to remove that siege of grief from her,
  Betrothed and would have married her perforce
  To County Paris. Then comes she to me,

  And with wild looks bid me devise some mean
  To rid her from this second marriage,   40
  Or in my cell there would she kill herself.

  Then gave I her (so tutored by my art)
  A sleeping potion, which so took effect
  As I intended, for it wrought on her

  The form of death. Mean time I writ to Romeo   45
  That he should hither come as this dire night
  To help to take her from her borrowed grave,
  Being the time the potion's force should cease.
  But he which bore my letter, Friar John,

  Was stayed by accident, and yesternight   50
  Returned my letter back. Then all alone,

At the prefixèd hour of her waking,
Came I to take her from her kindred's vault,
Meaning to keep her closely at my cell,
55 Till I conveniently could send to Romeo.
But when I came, some minute ere the time
Of her awakening, here untimely lay
The noble Paris and true Romeo dead.
She wakes, and I entreated her come forth
60 And bear this work of heaven with patience.
But then a noise did scare me from the tomb,
And she too desperate would not go with me,
But as it seems, did violence on herself.
All this I know, and to the marriage
65 Her nurse is privy; and if ought in this
Miscarried by my fault, let my old life
Be sacrificed, some hour before his time,
Unto the rigour of severest law.

PRINCE We still have known thee for a holy man.
70   Where's Romeo's man? what can he say to this?

BALTHASAR I brought my master news of Juliet's death,
And then in post he came from Mantua
To this same place, to this same monument.
This letter he early bid me give his father,
75 And threatened me with death, going in the vault,
If I departed not and left him there.

PRINCE Give me the letter, I will look on it.
Where is the County's page that raised the Watch?
Sirrah, what made your master in this place?

80 PAGE He came with flowers to strew his lady's grave,
And bid me stand aloof, and so I did.
Anon comes one with light to ope the tomb,
And by and by my master drew on him,
And then I ran away to call the Watch.

85 PRINCE This letter doth make good the Friar's words,
Their course of love, the tidings of her death;
And here he writes that he did buy a poison
Of a poor pothecary, and therewithal
Came to this vault to die, and lie with Juliet.
90 Where be these enemies? Capulet, Montague?
See what a scourge is laid upon your hate,
That heaven finds means to kill your joys with love!
And I for winking at your discords too
Have lost a brace of kinsmen. All are punished.

95 CAPULET O brother Montague, give me thy hand.
This is my daughter's jointure, for no more
Can I demand.

---

closely secretly
send send a message

this work of heaven God's will
from away from

is privy can testify
ought anything
Miscarried ... fault went wrong because of me
Unto ... law according to the full rigour of the law
still have have always

in post very quickly

raised called

Anon soon
drew on fought with

doth make good supports

See ... hate look what your hate has done
heaven God
to kill ... love to turn your children's happiness to sorrow (because of your hatred)
for winking at because of closing my eyes to
brace pair
jointure gift of friendship

'Poor sacrifices of our enmity'
(dir. Franco Zeffirelli, 1968)

MONTAGUE   But I can give thee more,
For I will raise her statue in pure gold,
That whiles Verona by that name is known,
There shall no figure at such rate be set   100
As that of true and faithful Juliet.

CAPULET As rich shall Romeo's by his lady's lie,
Poor sacrifices of our enmity!

PRINCE A glooming peace this morning with it brings,
The sun for sorrow will not show his head.   105
Go hence to have more talk of these sad things;
Some shall be pardoned, and some punishèd:
For never was a story of more woe
Than this of Juliet and her Romeo.

Exeunt omnes

That whiles as long as
figure ... set person be so highly
acclaimed

As rich ... lie I will erect Romeo's
statue next to her
sacrifices victims

Activities

1. Compare the present passage with a former trial scene
(Text 9), elaborating on parallels and variations.

2. Discuss functions and effects of Friar Lawrence's last speech.

3. Would you call the final scene a 'happy ending'?

4. Watch chapter 28 of the DVD. How would you characterise
the atmosphere in this final scene? How is this achieved?

5. The film ends with the same device it begins with. What is
the effect created here?

Review 1: Roger Ebert, 'Romeo + Juliet' (1996, dir. Baz Luhrmann)

I've seen Shakespeare done in drag. I've seen Richard III as a Nazi. I've seen *The Tempest* as science fiction and as a Greek travelogue. I've seen Prince Hal and Falstaff as homosexuals in Portland. I've seen *King Lear* as a samurai drama and *Macbeth* as a Mafia story, and
5 two different *Romeo and Juliets* about ethnic difficulties in Manhattan (*West Side Story* and *China Girl*), but I have never seen anything remotely approaching the mess that the new punk version of *Romeo + Juliet* makes of Shakespeare's tragedy.

The desperation with which it tries to "update" the play and make it
10 "relevant" is greatly depressing. In one grand but doomed gesture, writer-director Baz Luhrmann has made a film that (a) will dismay any lover of Shakespeare, and (b) bore anyone lured into the theater by promise of gang wars, MTV-style. This production was a very bad idea. [...]

15 Much of the dialogue is shouted unintelligibly, while the rest is recited dutifully, as in a high school production. Leonardo DiCaprio and Claire Danes are talented and appealing young actors, but they're in over their heads here. There is a way to speak Shakespeare's language so that it can be heard and understood, and they
20 have not mastered it. [...]

The film's climactic scenes are more impressed by action-movie clichés than by the alleged source. Romeo pumps Tybalt full of lead while shouting incomprehensible lines. He tenderly undresses Juliet and they spend the night together. Shakespeare's death scene
25 in the tomb lacked a dramatic payoff for Luhrmann, who has Juliet regain consciousness just as Romeo poisons himself, so that she can use her sweet alases while he can still hear them.

No doubt I will receive mail from readers accusing me of giving away the story's ending by revealing that Romeo and Juliet die. I had
30 my answer all prepared: If you do not already know what happens to the star-crossed lovers, then you are not the audience this movie is aiming for. But, stay, my pen! Perhaps you are.

Roger Ebert, *Romeo+Juliet*, www.rogerebert.com, 01.11.1996 [26.04.2016]

drag men wearing women's clothes
travelogue travel report

to dismay to disappoint
to lure to attract

unintelligibly impossible to understand

in over their heads unable to cope

alleged so-called
lead metal, *here:* bullet

alases sighs

Activities

1. Identify the main points of criticism the reviewer mentions.

2. What aspects do you agree/disagree with?

3. If you had not seen the film, would this review encourage you to go and see it? If so, why? If not, why not?

Review 2: Lyn Gardner, 'Romeo and Juliet' (Shakespeare's Globe, Review)

canoodling kissing
poignancy intensity

On a spring evening, love's young dream isn't just on stage, but also in the Globe's yard, where the sheer number of canoodling couples lends a poignancy to a revival that launches the 2009 season. Dominic Dromgoole's production initially set my heart aflutter, too. It's
5 got some good things going for it: clever use of music, a distinctly bustling Verona, and a Benvolio (Jack Farthing) and Mercutio (Philip Cumbus) whose puppyish high jinks hide more fragile uncertain-

jinks playfulness
bawdy vulgar, dirty

ties. Penny Layden's nurse is real flesh and blood, too, not the bawdy caricature of tradition.
10 But for all its initial urgency, and a beautifully staged ball scene where the young lovers first catch each other's eye, this evening, like

Ellie Kendrick and Adetomiwa Edun in Dominic Dromgoole's production of *Romeo and Juliet*, 2009

a great many love affairs, simply peters out. Its clarity is no substitute for real passion. Adetomiwa Edun's Romeo is clearly a nice lad, and might be more passionate if Ellie Kendrick's touchingly seri-
15 ous, doll-like Juliet showed a little more emotion.

The untrained Kendrick, making her stage debut at 18, always looks as if she would be happier on the lacrosse field than having wild sex in the bedroom. (That may be because the production is as hazy as to where Juliet's bedroom is located as it is about the entrance to the
20 Capulet vault.) Kendrick speaks the verse intelligently, but never convinces us there is a woman's heart swelling inside Juliet's 14-year-old body. The lovers greet each other's deaths with the slightly disappointed air of teenagers who have just heard they haven't done quite as well as expected in their chemistry A-levels. It is a very different
25 kind of chemistry that is lacking here.

Lyn Gardner, 'Romeo and Juliet, Shakespeare's Globe, Review', www.theguardian.com, 04.05.2009 [08.02.2016] Copyright Guardian News & Media Ltd 2016

peter out die out, fade

hazy blurred

swelling growing

Activities

1. What aspect of the play is emphasised most strongly in Lyn Gardner's review?

2. Compare the description of Ellie Kendrick and Adetomiwa Edun's portrayal of the lovers with that of Claire Danes and Leonardo DiCaprio in the film. Do you see any major differences?

3. Reflect on the differences between a stage and a film production – what has to be considered in each case?

Literary Glossary

Expression	Explanation
Alliteration	the repetition of sounds at the beginning of neighbouring words or stressed syllables, often used to underline the significance of the words in question or to emphasise a contrast between them: 'From forth the fatal loins of these two foes' (Text 1); 'Parting is such sweet sorrow' (Text 5).
Allusion	sth. said or written that refers to sth. else in an indirect way. The nurse is particularly fond of sexual allusions: 'women grow bigger by men' refers to pregnancy (Text 3); 'you shall bear the burden soon at night' hints at Juliet's forthcoming wedding night with Romeo (Text 7).
Ambiguity	expressions or statements having more than one meaning, often used to amuse partners or an audience, especially so in comedy. In tragedy the device more often serves to hide the truth or even to deceive a listener. Juliet's report on her one and only meeting with her undesired would-be bridegroom Paris is intended to calm down her father and to amuse the audience: 'I met the youthful lord … gave him what becomèd love I might, / Not stepping o'er the bound of modesty' (Text 13).
Antecedents (--'--)	from Latin *antecedere* = to go before, the events that took place before the actual opening of a play, a novel etc. Romeo's unrequited love for Rosaline is part of the antecedents of *Romeo and Juliet*.
Antagonism/ antagonist (-'---)	feeling of hatred and strong opposition. Tybalt is Romeo's antagonist. The Capulets and the Montagues are antagonistic families.
Antithesis (-'---)	the placing of a sentence or one of its parts against another to which it is opposed to form a balanced contrast: 'O serpent heart, hid with a flow'ring face!' (Text 10); 'I must be gone and live, or stay and die' (Text 11).
Aside	a remark or a short speech that is only addressed to the audience and, as a dramatic convention* cannot be heard by the other characters on stage. 'I would I knew not why it should be slowed' (Text 12).
Blank verse	unrhymed lines of ten syllables, usually patterned in iambic pentameters, derived from Greek *penta* = five and *iambus* = an unstressed syllable followed by a stressed one. So a regular blank verse runs like this: -x-x-x-x-x: 'The clock struck nine when I did send the Nurse' (Text 7). Quite often Shakespeare's lines are less regular than this one.
Caricature	from Italian *caricare* = to overload, exaggerate; a grotesque representation of a person or thing by exaggeration of characteristic traits. In Text 2 Romeo appears like a caricature of a Petrarchan* lover.

Expression	Explanation
Chorus	in ancient Greek drama there usually was a group of performers who gave comments, background and summary information on the play. The Prologue* may fulfill a similar function (Text 1).
Convention	a sort of agreement between the author and his audience to accept an element in a play or in another form of art that would appear improbable or even impossible in real life, e.g. an aside* or people talking in verse or singing an aria, after they have been stabbed in an opera, or an abstract painting etc.: 'I would I knew not why it should be slowed' (Text 12).
Dilemma	a situation involving an undesirable or unpleasant choice between two alternatives, none of which will lead to happiness or satisfaction. Examples: Romeo's separation from Juliet in their wedding night (Text 11) or Juliet before drinking the friar's mixture leading to her seeming death (Text 14).
Dramatic character	also dramatic figure or person acting in a play. Shakespeare's plays are crowded with such dramatic figures. They characterize themselves and other members of the stage-society* through their actions and – even more – through their words in dialogues and soliloquies*. There are principal or major characters, such as the titular figures, and minor ones, e.g. Balthasar, there are heroes and heroines, more or less sympathetic figures, comic and tragic ones.
Dramatic situation	the constellation of characters and their intentions on stage at a given moment of a play.
Elizabethan	referring to Elizabeth I (1533–1603), Queen of England 1558–1603. The so-called Elizabethan age marked the beginning of the British Empire, mainly based on the power of the navy, which defeated the Spanish Armada in 1588. The much-debated Elizabethan World Picture emphasized notions like order, stability, harmony and correspondences between the human world and the universe, microcosm and macrocosm. All this plays an important part in Shakespeare's plays, see e.g. the many sea images (Cf. hyperbole*, Text 5) or observations like 'The sun for sorrow will not show his head' (Text 17).
Genre	French for 'type' or 'kind'. Basically one can distinguish between three literary genres: epic, lyric and dramatic, all of them falling into many subcategories. Major dramatic forms are tragedy, comedy, history play. Shakespeare paid less attention to such distinctions than many other authors. He tended to mix literary genres or even to ridicule them. So there are quite a few comic elements in the tragedy of *Romeo and Juliet*, e.g. the character of the nurse, the clash between old age and youth in Text 6.
Hyperbole (-'---), adj.: hyperbolical (--'---)	an enormous exaggeration, often used by Shakespeare's characters to stress deep emotions: 'My bounty is as boundless as the sea, / My love as deep' (Text 5).
Imagery	language that produces pictures in the minds of an audience. Shakespeare's characters continually express themselves through images: 'O she does teach the torches to burn bright! / It seems she hangs upon the cheek of night / As a rich jewel in an Ethiop's ear' (Text 4).

Expression	Explanation
Metaphor	an image used without an adverb of comparison: 'Read o'er the volume of young Paris' face, / And find delight writ there with beauty's pen' (Text 3). A coherent cluster of metaphors is sometimes called an allegory*.
Monologue	often used as a synonym of soliloquy*. Some people prefer to use it for any long speech in a play or in everyday conversation. See e.g. the long reports given by Benvolio (Text 9) or by Friar Lawrence (Text 17).
Monosyllable	a word consisting of one syllable only. Shakespeare makes frequent use of such words. Sometimes whole lines consist of nothing but monosyllables. They may be very weighty and effective, expressing deep emotions: 'I have a faint cold fear thrills through my veins' (Text 14).
Paradox	the opposite of 'orthodox' = correct, corresponding to what is generally accepted. Both terms are derived from Greek, *para ten doxa* meaning contrary to generally accepted belief. A special case of this is the oxymoron*, a contradiction between noun and accompanying adjective: 'O loving hate ... heavy lightness, serious vanity ... bright smoke, cold fire, sick health' (Text 2).
Parallelism	a sentence or other speech unit in which corresponding elements have the same or similar structures: 'Is Romeo slaughtered? and is Tybalt dead?' (Text 10).
Petrarchan	adj. referring to Francesco Petrarca (1304–1374); see caricature* and sonnet*.
Plot	the series of events which form the story of a novel, play, film etc. Shakespeare's plays have sometimes several plots. *Romeo and Juliet* is focussed very much on the main plot, centring around the tragic young couple. The old feud between the Capulets and the Montagues might be considered as a kind of sub-plot.
Prologue	an introductory scene or speech, preceding the opening act of a play. It may resemble a chorus (Text 1).
Rhetoric ('---)	the effective presentation of ideas in speech or writing. At medieval and early modern universities, rhetoric – based on classical Roman teaching – was an important discipline. Every educated person was trained to express their arguments in the style appropriate for the subject matter. The aim of the rhetorician (--'--) was to convince his audience of his arguments, which meant that he had to work on their intellect as well as on their emotions and imagination.
Scene	a unit of action in which there is no change of place nor any interval in time. During a Shakespearean scene there are often entrances and exits of characters, meaning changes in the stage-society* and usually introducing new phases in a scene.
Setting	generally speaking the background against which the action takes place. It may include the period of time, society, ethnic or religious framework, country, landscape etc. In a more restricted sense it means the place in which a scene* is acted out.

Expression	Explanation
Soliloquy	(-'---) derived from Latin *solus* and *loqui* = to speak alone. A character is alone on the stage and – seemingly talking to himself – reveals his inner thoughts, feelings, plans etc. to the audience. Like an aside*, this is a dramatic convention* very popular in medieval drama and still quite frequent in Shakespeare's plays, especially when a character finds himself in a dilemma or before an important decision (Texts 14 and 15).
Sonnet	from the Italian 'sonetto' = a little sound, song or poem. It originated in 13th century Italy. Most outstanding early Italian sonneteers, i.e. authors of sonnets, were Dante Alighieri (1264–1321) and above all Francesco Petrarca (1304–1374), in English Petrarch. His sonnets consisted of two quatrains (= one octave) and two tercets (= one sestet), usually following the rhyme scheme abba abba cdc cdc, sometimes cde cde etc. In most of his sonnets he adored a married lady who was unobtainable to him. This created a long tradition of sonnets addressed to stone-hearted ladies who never fulfilled their lovers' desire. The English sonnet normally consists of three quatrains and a concluding couplet, with the rhyme scheme abab cdcd efef gg. In his unrequited love for Rosaline, Romeo first appears as a kind of caricature* of a Petrarchan lover. Text 1 and the first dialogue between Romeo and Juliet (Text 4) are sonnets of the English kind.
Stage-direction	instruction to directors and actors indicating entrances, exits, music, gestures etc. One can distinguish between direct stage directions which are not spoken by the actors and indirect ones which are part of the spoken texts and usually refer to other characters on the stage. Text 16 contains a number of both kinds.
Stage-society	the ensemble of characters on stage at a given moment of a play. In a more general sense: all the characters appearing during a play.
Stichomythia	a dialogue in which the alternating speeches consist of single lines, expressing excitement or antagonism* and creating an effect of high tension* or – in comic dialogues – of quick-wittedness and amusement (Text 12: Juliet vs. Paris).
Stratagem	a trick or plan to gain advantage over others. The intention may be benevolent or evil. In tragedies malevolent or evil tricks, schemes or plots are usually employed to do serious damage to an opponent. In comedies stratagems are often intended to help friends in difficult situations.
Tension and suspense	these terms have overlapping meanings and are usually translated by one and the same word into German. In English one should differentiate: tension exits between opposing forces or individuals, e.g. between the Capulets and the Montagues or between Tybalt and Romeo. Suspense, on the other hand, implies a feeling of uncertainty about what is going to happen next. It is rather typical of detective stories, action films and also of Shakespeare's plays.
Villain	a person capable of great wickedness, the principal bad character in a play whose evil actions or motives are important to the plot*. Most famous Shakespearean villains are the Duke of Gloucester in *King Richard III*, Iago in *Othello* or Edmund in *King Lear*. These are almost caricatures* of villains. They are even proud of their crimes and relish in their misdeeds. *Romeo and Juliet* is rather untypical, as there is no villain in this tragedy.

Film Analysis Glossary[1]

Expression	Explanation
Camera angle	the camera creates the frame, which strongly influences the story. This also depends on the perspective the camera takes, which results from the angle in which it is pointed, e.g. from above, from below etc.
Camera movement	the way the camera moves influences the story in the sense that through quick movements, for example, suspense may be achieved.
Cinemato-graphy	the combination of camera movements, shots, angles, and lighting.
Close-up	the camera is very close to its object, for example a character's face, so that it is clearly visible in detail (e.g. facial expressions). This way the object gains importance for the story.
Cuts	after the film has been shot, it is cut, so that the length of scenes is altered. Many cuts, i.e. quickly alternating scenes, can create suspense (for example in so-called 'action films').
Diegetic	the term comes from *diegesis*, which means 'story'. The diegetic level of a film (or novel) is where the story takes place. If, for instance, on the diegetic level of a film music is played, the characters can hear and comment on it. If the music is on the extradiegetic level, as it often is at the beginning of the film, it is not supposed to be understood as being played in the world of the story.
Editing	after a film is shot, it is cut, scenes are re-arranged, music and sound effects are added etc. The whole process is called editing.
Exposition	in classical drama, the first of five acts is called the exposition. In film, this means the first sequence, which can have a variety of lengths. In the exposition, the main characters, the main themes, the setting, the circumstances etc. are introduced.
Extreme close-up	the camera is so close that only part of the person or object are captured in the frame. This shot is used to highlight such tiny details as, for example, someone's eyes.
Flashforward	in contrast to the flashback, the flashforward reveals events in the film that might (but don't have to) occur in the future of the story.
Frame	the camera creates the frame for everything we see on the screen at a given moment, which is one single image.

[1] see also Close-Up. The Language of Film from A–Z, ed. Olaf Schneider, Schöningh, Paderborn 2011

Expression	Explanation
High-angle shot	the camera is pointed at a character or object so that we look at them, as if we were above them.
Lighting	the light a director uses is a very important means for interpreting the story and creating various moods (e.g. fear through dark lighting).
Medium close-ups	a shot which shows a little bit more than a close-up. In addition to a person's head this shot also captures the shoulders and parts of the upper body.
Mise-en-scène	the French term literally means 'put on the scene'. It refers to anything that can be seen in the frame at a given moment in the film.
Motif	in film, as well as in drama and narrative, a motif is a certain theme that occurs numerous times throughout the story and has symbolic significance.
Props	any object that is used for the story or the actors, such as clothes, furniture, settings etc., is called props (both in film and on stage).
Setting	in film, the setting is the location in which the action takes place. This does not necessarily have to be a real geographical place but can be specifically designed for the film.
Shot	the image the camera shoots like a photo camera.
Slow motion	an action appears slower than normal, as if time is slowed down for a moment.
Sound	the sound of a film can have two functions: it may occur on the diegetic level, like the sound a character makes by moving around in the setting; or it can be added by the editor afterwards, such as music.
Still	a single frame of a film, very much like a photo.
Tracking shot	'tracking' means 'moving' in this case: the camera may follow moving characters or objects around.
Voiceover	a voice that is not part of the narrative/diegetic level.
Zoom	adjusting the lens of the camera so that objects seem closer than they actually are. Through such a close focus, characters etc. may gain importance in the story.

Acknowledgements

© picture alliance/United Archives/WHA: p. 4 l.; © Kobal/FOTOFINDER.COM: p. 4 r.; © Arsenal/SammlungRichter: p. 5; © picture alliance: p. 6; © Twentieth Century Fox: p. 7, p. 9, p. 13, p. 14, p. 26, p. 36, p. 39, p. 42; © Paramount: p. 11, p. 21, p. 24, p. 28, p. 30, p. 33, p. 37, p. 43, p. 44, p. 48; © Metro-Goldwyn-Mayer Studios Inc.: p. 18; © picture alliance/ Photoshot: p. 50; others: Verlagsarchiv Schöningh